MACHINE APPLIQUÉ

MACHINE APPLIQUÉ

Sharon Perna

Sterling Publishing Co., Inc.   New York

EDITED BY BARBARA BUSCH

Library of Congress Cataloging-in-Publication Data

Perna, Sharon.
  Machine appliqué.

  Includes index.
  1. Machine appliqué.   I. Title.
TT779.P47 1986   746.44'5   86-14419
ISBN 0-8069-4774-8
ISBN 0-8069-4776-4 (pbk.)

Published by Sterling Publishing Co., Inc.
387 Park Avenue South, New York, N.Y. 10016
Distributed in Canada by Sterling Publishing
% Canadian Manda Group, P.O. Box 920, Station U
Toronto, Ontario, Canada M8Z 5P9
Distributed in Great Britain and Europe by Cassell PLC
Artillery House, Artillery Row, London SW1P 1RT, England
Distributed in Australia by Capricorn Ltd.
P.O. Box 665, Lane Cove, NSW 2066

CONTENTS

This book is dedicated to three special loved ones—to my husband, Richard Dennis, and to my parents, Edwannah and Charles Perna

INTRODUCTION

Machine appliqué is one of the most exciting and challenging of needlecraft activities. It has given me so many hours of enjoyment and satisfaction that I wanted to share my expertise and techniques with each of you.

Machine Appliqué is written as a how-to book for the beginner as well as the seasoned sewer. The methods presented here are practical, informative, and based on ten years of my appliquéing experience. With a text that carries both general and very specific information, you should be able to learn the techniques of machine appliqué through a combination of reading, inspecting lots of diagrams, and viewing contemporary examples. Then, once you have mastered the basics, the full-sized appliqué patterns grouped at the end of the book will get you going on appealing projects that are appropriate for your level of skill.

If you think that machine appliqué might interest you, consider the versatility of this craft. For the design, the fabrics, the combination of sewing techniques (mixed with embroidery, quilting, and trapunto), and the surfaces being decorated can be varied to suit an almost infinite number of tastes. This is truly a needle art where there is something for everyone and all levels of sewing abilities can be satisfied and thrilled. Now it is my pleasure to introduce this timeless craft to you—or possibly new aspects of it.

THE BEGINNINGS

Appliqué is a word derived from the French. It can be either a verb or a noun. As a verb it means to put on, to apply, or to attach one material to another by sewing. As a noun it refers to the cloth cutout shape or shapes, which form a type of surface decoration. The design which results can be as simple as a single shape or as complicated as a jigsaw puzzle.

There are two types of machine appliqué. There is a machine appliqué with the raw edges left flat and covered by machine satin-stitching, and there is a machine appliqué with a seam allowance turned back and edged in a machine satin-stitch. Each method has its own advantages and disadvantages. Both share many similarities. However, before discussing them in depth, it is necessary to turn to the beginning and that leads us to planning the design.

Designing

As an art form, machine appliqués are usually simple, bold, and stylized. Typical designs are birds, flowers, animals, leaves, hearts, wreaths, and other flowing shapes. Often they reflect personal interests and hobbies as well as special occasions and celebrations of life.

Since drawing and planning a design may be the most difficult part in the entire appliqué process, the back of the book contains numerous pages of suitable full-size line drawings. If, however, after using the patterns furnished, your creativity is sparked to the extent that you want to produce your own designs, the following tips might be helpful:

1. *Work from your own personal photos.* Select either black-and-white or color photos (3½″ × 5″, 5″ × 7″, or 8″ × 10″) with simple lines, gradual curves, and shapes of a good size. Place a sheet of tracing paper on top

of the photo. With pencil trace over the entire shape, so that you have a simplified line drawing. Remove the tracing. Compare the drawing to the photo. Rework or complete any unfinished portion of the design.

2. *Draw from nature.* Sketch the plant forms, animal life, and natural phenomenon around you as line drawings. Then consider abstracting, dissecting, magnifying, or silhouetting the sketches you have made. Have faith in your drawing abilities and a willingness to experiment. Like any other ability, practice makes perfect.

If sketching on a piece of fresh white paper terrifies you, save grocery or shopping bags, newsprint, pieces of tracing paper, cardboard, and wrapping paper. If you make mistakes on these surfaces, it will not matter, and your willingness to draw will not be crushed.

3. *Save magazine photos and decorative floor, wall, and home-furnishing catalogues.* If you are interested in particular subjects and shapes, start saving and organizing these pictures in folders. At the appropriate time use this reference material to suggest your theme or variation. Draw directly from the clippings.

4. *Use the drawings and paintings of your children.* Even if you are afraid to draw, you may have children who have that glorious freedom to express their ideas. Instead of hanging their pictures on the refrigerator or kitchen bulletin board, ask if you can transform their artwork into appliqués. Choose large, simple designs which have meaning to you and your children.

Making the Master Pattern

Once you have worked out your design, redraw it in the center of a sheet of tracing paper (Illus. 1), using pencil. Take a second sheet of tracing paper and draw the seam lines and cutting lines of the shape that will carry the design (Illus. 2). Place the tracing of the shape over

cutting lines

stitching lines

Illus. 1 (left). Design centered on tracing paper.

Illus. 2 (right). Pillow-front tracing.

the design, and move the appliqué to the most pleasing position (Illus. 3). Then ask yourself the following questions: Is this design the right size for the article? Is this the best position for the appliqué? Is this design suitable for the object and the space? If so, draw your design within the tracing of the object. From this point on, call this full-size tracing the master pattern (Illus. 4).

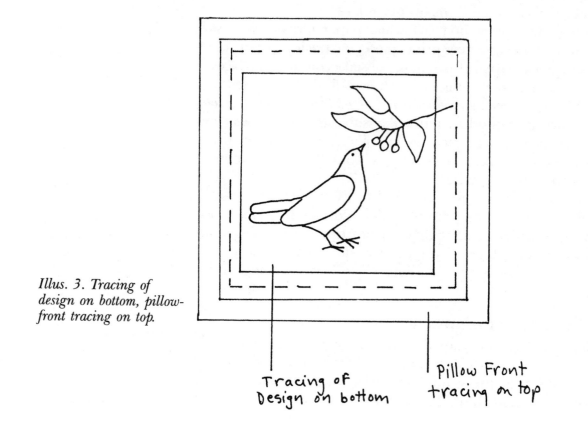

Illus. 3. Tracing of design on bottom, pillow-front tracing on top.

Tracing of
Design on bottom

Pillow Front
tracing on top

Illus. 4. Master pattern.

If the design looks too large or too small, consult the enlarging and reducing instructions that follow to produce a revised drawing. Slip this new line drawing back under the tracing of the shape and continue as usual.

The importance of the master pattern cannot be overstated. It is a kind of architectural blueprint which has several functions: 1. It carries the full-size design in its proper position on the supporting shape; 2. It is used to make the patterns for the individual appliqué shapes; 3. It is used to register each part of the appliqué in its correct position on the background, and; 4. It carries the numerical sequence and colors selected for each part of the appliqué. The master pattern is for reference only and should not be cut up.

Enlarging or Reducing the Design

When a black-and-white line drawing needs to be enlarged or reduced, the easiest thing to do is to take the design to a business with a Photostat copy machine. The cost of the "blow-up" or the "reduction" depends on the size of the finished product. Since most Photostat machines do not have paper rollers that exceed 24 inches in width, there are recognizable limits to the equipment.

The other way to enlarge or reduce a design is called the grid method, i.e., small squares are superimposed over the design. For this method, follow these instructions.

1. Measure the widest part of the design. With tracing paper, ruler, and pencil, make a square this size, and it must be square. Center the square over the design and retrace the figure within the square (Illus. 5).

2. Fold the tracing in half across its width and then across its length (Illus. 6).

3. Open the tracing and fold it in quarters across its width and length.

Illus. 5 left.

Illus. 6 right.

With ruler and pencil draw over the folds to clearly define the sixteen squares (Illus. 7).

4. On a second piece of tracing paper, draw another square that is the size you want.

5. Fold it just as you folded the original square. Pencil in the lines. As an aid, you can, on both papers, number the corresponding squares from 1 to 16.

6. Place the two grids side by side. With pencil and eraser, copy the design square by square (Illus. 8). If any block in the grid seems too

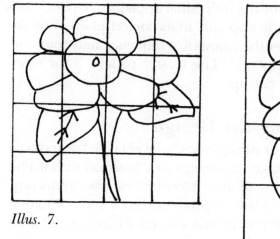

Illus. 7.

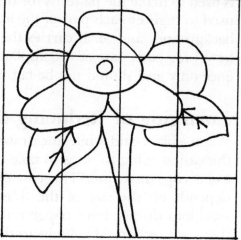

Illus. 8.

complicated to draw freehand, subdivide that block into fourths on the original and the finished tracing.

7. Check the final squared drawing to see that it is accurate.

Deciding on the Appliqué Sequence

Once the master pattern is made, it needs to be studied and analyzed to decide how many shapes there are in the design and in what order the shapes should be appliquéd. If you are building a scene, you will need to decide: Are there elements that need to go in the background to create distance? Are there elements that need to be placed in the foreground or midground to create the illusion of closeness? If your appliqué consists of several shapes, remember that large areas are applied first, and details are sewn on top even if this involves many layers of fabric.

When you are figuring out how many shapes there are in the appliqué, there is one exception to the rule. Sometimes you will have a background shape that spans both sides of the top shape, as, for example, the sun behind a tree limb (Illus. 9). In this instance, treat the sun as one complete uninterrupted circle (Illus. 10). Do not cut it in two pieces (Illus. 11). As a result, the design will have a neater appearance with less stitching under the limb.

After you have decided on the numerical order of your appliqué, translate your decisions into numbers from one on up. Pencil these numbers within the corresponding shapes on the master pattern (Illus. 12).

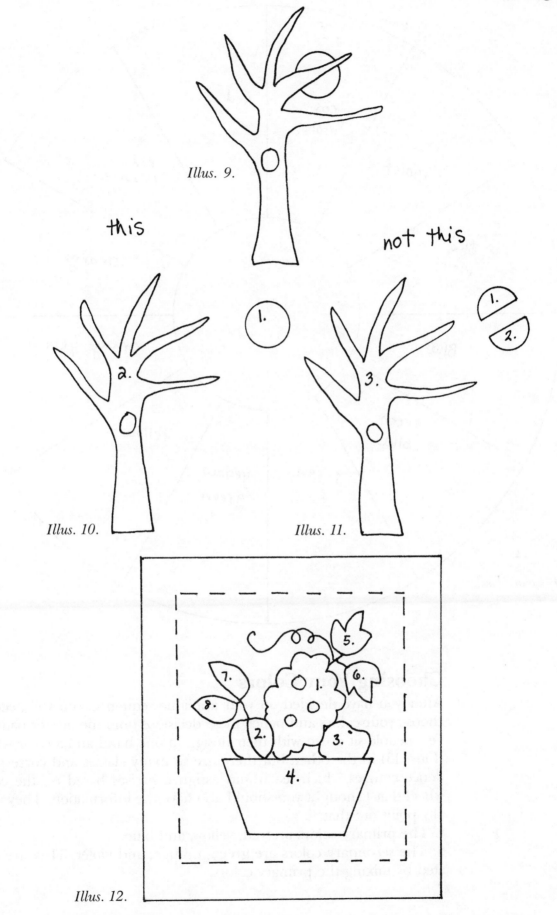

Illus. 9.

this

not this

Illus. 10.

Illus. 11.

Illus. 12.

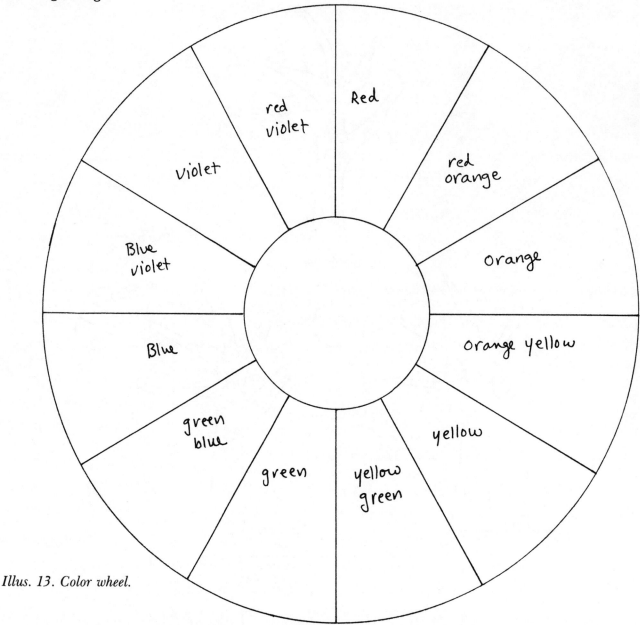

Illus. 13. Color wheel.

Choosing Your Colors

After you have decided on your appliqué sequence, you will need to choose your colors and pencil these decisions onto the master pattern. Few people sit down with their design in one hand and a color wheel (Illus. 13) in the other, but there are so many classes and correspondence courses which teach and assign exercises based on the color wheel that I thought you should also have the information. They usually point out that:

1. The primary colors are red, yellow, and blue.
2. The secondary colors are green, orange, and violet. They are created by mixing the primary colors.

3. The tertiary colors are red-orange, orange-yellow, yellow-green, green-blue, blue-violet, and red-violet. They are created by mixing a primary and a secondary color.

4. An achromatic color scheme has values from white to black and includes a number of greys.

5. A monochromatic color scheme has a number of the lights and darks of one color, as a combination of reds.

6. A neutral color scheme is one of whites, blacks, greys, or beiges. This plan has little color.

7. A polychromatic color scheme has a wide range of colors.

8. A complementary color scheme has the lights and darks of colors which lie opposite each other on the color wheel as, for example, a picture with blue and orange or purple and yellow.

There is no doubt that exercises using these color combinations will expand your fabric palette. Being adventuresome and having an inquiring attitude also helps. However, I would also suggest supplementing this information with the start of a color file which can be used for future reference. In it you might include the following:

Swatches. Save fabrics, wallpaper samples, and pieces of wrapping paper that have interesting and pleasing color combinations. You might also try swapping small squares of your favorite color schemes with your friends.

Photos. Lots of people photograph historic monuments, their families, holidays, and all kinds of vacation activities. Why not use your camera to capture color combinations that are found in nature? Just open your eyes to the things around you, and capture those special colors on film.

Cards, calendars, and post cards. Collect beautiful and striking examples of commercially produced cards and stationery. Notice the traditional color combinations used for holidays, seasons, and special events, as well as the symbolic use of certain colors.

Notes. Take notes on color schemes that excite you. Jot down these brief statements on index cards, and try to duplicate these recipes sometime in the future.

Making the Appliqué Patterns

Before the individual appliqué patterns can be made, it is important to understand the principle of overlap or lapover. Stated briefly, whenever two areas of appliqué touch (Illus. 14), the bottom shape has

Illus. 14.

approximately ¼″ or more extra fabric added to it (Illus. 15). This margin of safety is added for two reasons: First, the machine satin-stitching cannot span two fabrics without a lot of unravelling, and second, it prevents the bottom fabric from showing through in unwanted areas.

Illus. 15.

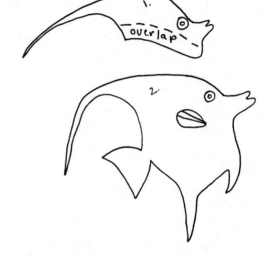

In the machine appliqué-without-seams method, the individual appliqué patterns are cut to size, and they do not have seam allowances added. In the machine appliqué-with-seams method, the individual appliqué patterns have a ¼″ or ⅛″ seam allowance added to each individual shape. Lapover areas can exist in both methods.

To make your appliqué patterns, place a sheet of tracing paper over the master pattern. As you work in the numerical sequence established on the master pattern, trace around the outline of each shape and include any inner details. Add, if necessary, the lapover areas and the seam allowances. Use a pencil and leave about ½″ between each pattern (Illus. 16 and 17).

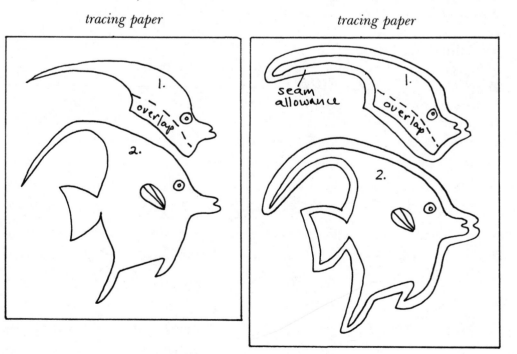

Illus. 16. Machine-appliqué-without-seams method.

Illus. 17. Machine-appliqué-with-seams method.

Laying Out the Pattern

To prevent puckering and stretching, your appliqué and background patterns need to be positioned in the same manner on each piece of fabric. You can place your patterns on either the straight grain (lengthwise grain) of the fabric or on the crosswise grain. Stated briefly, the straight grain of the fabric runs parallel to the selvage (Illus. 18) and has hardly any stretch; the crosswise grain runs at right angles to the selvage (Illus. 19) and will stretch, but the amount is minuscule. The bias or the diagonal stretches the most (Illus. 20) and should be completely avoided for appliqué.

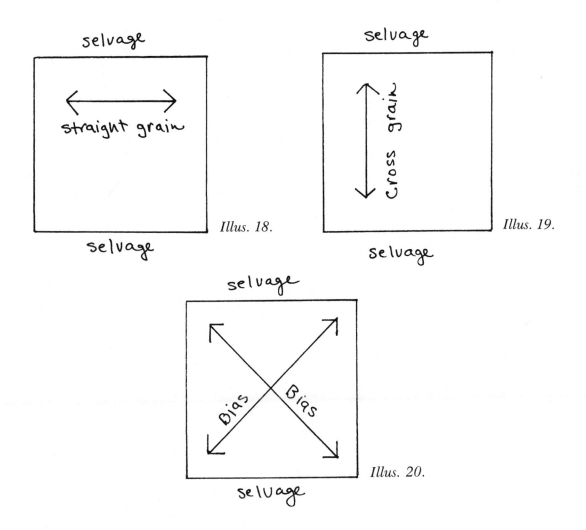

Illus. 18.

Illus. 19.

Illus. 20.

FABRIC

In most appliqués, it is easy to figure out the yardage. Usually the appliqué itself uses small bits of different colored fabrics, and you can find what is necessary in your own collection of scraps. If, however, you are doing a large coordinating project such as four place mats decorated with the theme of a rooster weather vane, you will need to map out the cutting arrangement on paper to calculate the yardage.

Since most fabrics come in a width of 45″, draw a rectangle and label the width. Decide if you will be cutting your shapes on the straight or crosswise grain. Then measure the length and width of each individual pattern (including seam allowances) and for the sake of mapping out, simplify the pattern shapes into rectangles, squares, circles, or triangles. On your paper rectangle fill in the pattern pieces to be cut from the same fabric leaving ¼ to 1″ between the different shapes. To determine the length of the fabric you will need, add up the inches and throw in an extra ⅛ or ¼ yard as a margin of safety. Divide the total by 36 and for the inches that remain, round off the yardage so that you are purchasing ⅛, ¼, ⅜, ½, ⅝, ¾, or ⅞ yard (Illus. 21–24).

Selecting the Fabrics

When you have worked out your color scheme and calculated your yardage, you will have to select the fabrics that come closest to your plans. Most machine appliqué projects are made with 100% cottons or cotton blends. Cotton is an ideal natural fabric. It comes in different widths and weights; it offers a good supply of solids and prints; it ravels and stretches less than blends; and it is easily laundered. Dress-weight cottons such as bleached and unbleached muslin (calico), broadcloth, kettle cloth, poplin, denim, corduroy, trigger, and sailcloth are all good for both the appliqué and the background. Full polyesters, knits, and

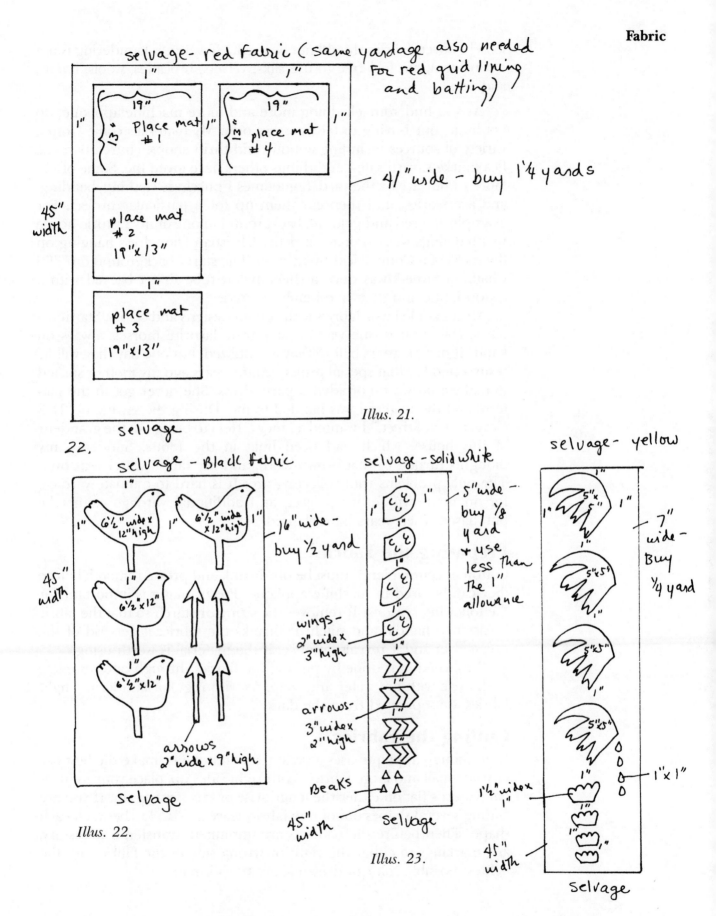

selvage- red fabric (same yardage also needed
for red grid lining
and batting)

1"

1"

19"

Place mat
1

13"

1"

19"

M

place mat
4

1"

41" wide - buy 1¼ yards

45"
width

1"

place mat
2

19"x 13"

1"

place mat
3

19"x13"

selvage

Illus. 21.

22.

selvage - Black fabric

selvage -solid white

selvage- yellow

1"

1"

1"

1"

1"

5"x
5"

1"

6½" wide x
12"high

6½" wide
x 12"high

1"

16" wide -
buy ½ yard

5" wide -
buy ⅛
yard
+ use
less than
the 1"
allowance

5"x5"

7"
wide -
Buy
¼ yard

45"
width

1"

6½" x 12"

5"x5"

1"

6½"x12"

wings -
2" wide x
3" high

5"x5"

arrows
2" wide x 9" high

arrows -
3" wide x
2" high

1"

0
0
0
0

1" x 1"

selvage

Beaks

1½" wide x
1"

Illus. 22.

45"
width

selvage

45"
width

selvage

Illus. 23.

Illus. 24.

25

loosely woven fabrics should not be used. However, if laundering is not a consideration, feel free to use silks, velvets, brocades, wools, linens, and felts.

As you find yourself doing more and more machine appliqué, do not limit your buying to fabric stores only. My materials come from a variety of sources including antique and thrift shops, church bazaars, flea markets, yard sales, and things others have given me. Some of the fabrics I buy are by the yard. Sometimes I purchase clothing, bedding, and accessories, and then cut them up for a particular project. For example, the red and gold silk background in one of my historic-house wall hangings was originally a petite Christian Dior dress hanging on the racks of a Connecticut thrift shop. The starry background on "309 Chatham Street" was once a sheer nylon robe that I backed with a cotton fabric and then hand-embroidered.

Most people favor fabrics with certain designs and colors. Starting a fabric collection is one way to have your favorite morsels always on hand. It may be years before they are utilized, but one day they will be resurrected for that special project. Many years ago my mother started to make a brown embroidered party dress. She never got to the pattern, and the material was handed to me. During the sewing of "1118 Government Street," I wanted a fancy taffeta to bring out the grandeur of this house, which had been built in the 1860's. Suddenly, my thoughts turned to that brown cloth, and my fabric search was over. The only problems with collecting are: It is hard to estimate yardage for an unknown future project, and additional yardage cannot be purchased when years have elapsed.

Preparing the Fabrics

Cotton or cotton blends must be preshrunk and pressed smooth before they can be used in machine appliqué. Preshrinking is important for the following reasons: It removes the sizing or starch so that the fabric is easier to handle and stitch; it shrinks the fabric; it gets rid of the excess dye; and it reveals, at once, if the material is worth using.

Preshrinking is done by putting the fabrics through one complete wash cycle with hot water and soap. As with regular laundering, light fabrics are separated from the dark.

Cutting the Fabrics

Even though appliqué uses a great many remnants, make the best use of your small and large fabrics. With right sides up, place your individual patterns flat on either the lengthwise or crosswise grain. If you are cutting several shapes out of one fabric, leave a ¼″ to ½″ between each shape. Then before the patterns are unpinned, transfer, if necessary, any markings to either the right or wrong side of the fabric with the lightest possible color of dressmaker's tracing paper.

TOOLS
AND MATERIALS

The sewing machine is, of course, your most important tool. It is not necessary to have a fancy top-of-the-line machine, but you do need a zigzag machine that can produce a smooth satin stitch. On my model the straight-stitch foot is replaced with a satin-stitch foot, sometimes called the appliqué presser foot (Illus. 25 and 26). I also have a stitch-width control with the numbers 1 to 4 (Illus. 27). This dialable control regulates the width of the satin stitch, i.e., the higher the number, the wider the stitch.

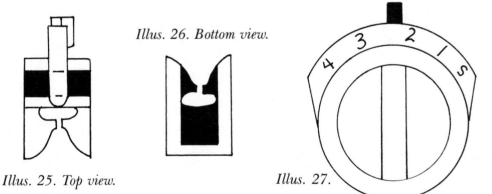

Illus. 26. Bottom view.

Illus. 25. Top view.

Illus. 27.

Because of the sewing machine's importance, it must be properly maintained with oiling (not household oil), dusting, and cleaning. In machine appliqué, lint constantly accumulates in the area around the bobbin and the feed dogs. If the lint is not removed frequently, your satin stitch will have many irregularities. Clean out this area with either the lint brush provided by the manufacturer or a soft, old toothbrush.
Needles. A sharp needle is necessary for a smooth even satin stitch. Never use a needle with a blunt point or one that is bent. For appliqués utilizing light- to medium-weight cottons, cotton blends, linens, or wools, a size 14 ballpoint machine needle works well. For appliqués

using heavy cottons such as corduroy, denim, or wool, change to a size 16 ballpoint needle.

Straight Pins. Buy those with the colored ball heads. Discard them when they are no longer rust-free and sharp.

Threads. Avoid those cheap bargain polyester threads piled high in the baskets in front of the shop's cash register. Polyester builds up static and causes a lot of stitching problems. Instead, use either 100% cotton thread or cotton-covered (wrapped) polyester for machine satin-stitching and general hand-sewing.

Tracing Paper. Get into the habit of using tracing paper for sketching and making the master and individual appliqué patterns. It has an excellent erasing quality, and the transparency is helpful in cutting out your fabrics and registering each part of the design in its proper position. This translucent paper comes in pads (9″ × 12″, 11″ × 14″, and 18″ × 24″) or in rolls (10 yards × 36″ wide and 50 yards × 36″ wide). It can be purchased in either a white or a yellowish color. The light and medium weights are fine for appliqué.

Polyester Batting. Poly-fil traditional needle-punched batting is available in seamless sheets of various sizes (crib—45″ × 60″, twin—72″ × 90″, full—81″ × 96″, and queen—90″ × 108″). It is nonallergenic, washable, and cuts like a fabric. If you are working with dark materials, however, watch out for polyester fibres, which can work their way through to the surface of the design. These loose wisps can produce an undesirable linty look.

Dressmaker's Tracing Paper (Washable and Dry-Cleanable). Dressmaker's tracing paper is used to transfer pattern markings to either the right or wrong side of the fabric. Although each packet contains an assortment of coated papers, use the white sheets whenever possible. White markings disappear easily with either the heat from the iron or soap and water. For light- and medium-colored fabrics, select the lightest possible color of dressmaker's tracing paper. For the best results, test

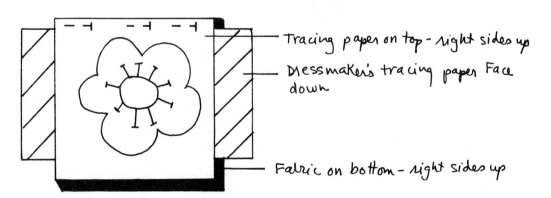

Tracing paper on top - right sides up

Dressmaker's tracing paper Face down

Fabric on bottom - right sides up

Illus. 28. For markings transferred to right side of fabric (the entire flower).

the carbon markings on a scrap of the fabric to make sure that the lines do not remain after washing.

Tools and Materials

When marking the fabric, always place the waxy side of the paper next to the cloth that is to be marked. Work on a hard surface, such as a sheet of glass or Formica laminated plastic for darker cleaner lines. Trace over the markings in the pattern with either a pencil or tracing wheel, and use just enough pressure to enable you to clearly see the marks (Illus. 28 and 29).

Illus. 29. For markings transferred to wrong side of fabric (the stitching lines).

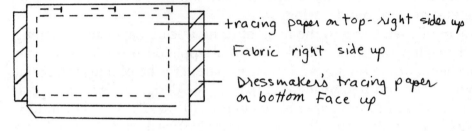

tracing paper on top-right sides up

Fabric right side up

Dressmaker's tracing paper on bottom face up

THE GALLERY

The examples that follow are meant to be an inspiration for the needlecraft you will do tomorrow. Use the artwork as a catalyst to suggest future possibilities and a springboard to start the flow of your own creative ideas. Remember, also, that these projects illustrate only a small portion of the enormous potential hidden within this craft. There are still so many other ideas beneath the tip of the iceberg.

As you look at the examples that I have selected, use the photos in the following manner: (1) Inspect the various color combinations; (2) notice the use of the fabrics and threads; (3) observe the interpretation of the themes and inspect the use of the various sewing techniques incorporated within the design; (4) examine the types of surfaces that can be decorated; and (5) study how the projects are finished off.

Unless stated otherwise, most of these projects have been made with cotton and cotton blends. To avoid repetitive phrases, all the artwork uses the technique of machine appliqué without seams unless stated otherwise. Comments are made whenever something special needs to be said.

Renaissance Man

Banner
33 by 42 inches
Plus quilting (the stitching follows the stripes in the man's tunic, the edges of the two rectangular insets, and forms scattered stars across the background)
Notice the treatment on the top and bottom of the banner. Appliquéd tabs, fringe, and exposed sections of wood can complement and enhance certain themes.

Renaissance Man (banner)

Ariel of Maine (banner)

*American Eagle (quilted jacket)
and Track Shoes (tote bag)*

Garden Basket (wall hanging)

Heart and Dove (wall hanging)

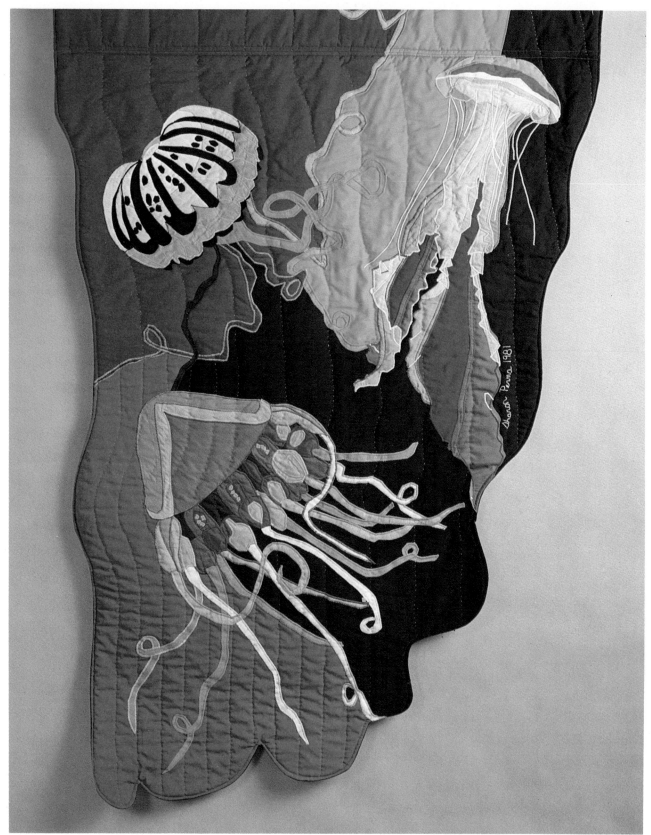

Jellyfish (banner)

Opposite page: Top, Pelicans (wall hanging); Octopus and Squid (quilted jacket) and Starfish (vest); Shell (wall hanging)

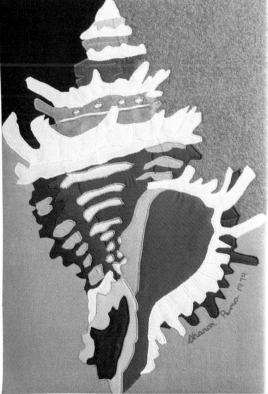

309 Chatham Street (wall hanging)

Wisconsin Calf and Calico Stove (pillows)

Rooster Weather Vane (place mat, table runner, chair cushion, tea cozy, and wall hanging)

1123 Palmetto Street (wall hanging)

Calico Rooster (wall hanging), Calico Swan (place mat)
and Tulips (place mat)

Angels (Christmas tree skirt)

Top: Flower Girl's Basket and Ring Bearer's Pillow
Left: Amaryllis (wall hanging)
Above: Spring Bouquet (wall hanging)

The Ariel of Maine

Banner
43 by 42 inches
Plus quilting (parallel lines pattern)
This clipper ship had a great deal of detail in the sails, rigging, and curly penmanship of the name. To capture all these fancy accents, narrow lines were machine-straight-stitched, wider lines were machine-satin-stitched, once or twice in various widths, and the name and year of the ship were machine-satin-stitched with many starts, stops, and tying off of threads.

American Eagle

Quilted Woman's Jacket
Commercial pattern plus embroidery (feather, satin, and running stitch), trapunto, and machine-straight-stitching
This jacket was given a sculptural quality by stuffing the eagle from the top side with different amounts of polyester fibre. The bird is also a good example of a subject that uses traditional colors (red, white, and blue) to further emphasize a theme. I used it on a jacket, but this particular design would do very nicely for a medallion quilt.

Track Shoes

Tote Bag
12 by 13 inches
First seen in *Needlecraft for Today*, July/August 1984

Garden Basket

Wall Hanging
31 by 32 inches
Plus quilting (the muslin blocks are filled with a diamond pattern and there is stitching within the calico borders) and piecing
First seen in *Needlecraft for Today*, September/October 1983.

Heart and Dove

Wall Hanging
30 by 30 inches
Plus quilting (within the hearts and gingham borders) and piecing
First seen in *Country Handcrafts*, Winter 1983.

Jellyfish

Banner
34 by 50 inches
Plus quilting (which follows the wavy contours of the banner)

In machine appliqué the thread normally matches the predominant color of each fabric. But to emphasize and exaggerate the iridescent colors of the jellyfish, I edged the pale blue, white, and brown tentacles with brighter and darker shades of blue, navy, rust, lavender, and beige.

Pelicans
Wall Hanging
40 by 32 inches
Plus embroidery (stem, single running, and feather stitch) and machine-straight-stitching

Octopus and Squid
Quilted Woman's Jacket
Commercial pattern plus quilting (parallel-line pattern)

Starfish
Woman's Vest
Polyester satins
Commercial pattern plus embroidery (straight, satin, cross, French knots, feather, running, and laced running stitch)
Notice how the embroidery covers and extends beyond the machine-satin-stitching, which is now almost invisible.

Shell
Wall Hanging
18 by 26 inches
Plain and textured cottons, corduroy, wools, and maxi-piping
Not every wall hanging needs a custom frame. Sometimes the soft edges of a design mounted over canvas stretcher bars are pleasant enough.

309 Chatham Street
Wall Hanging
30 by 24 inches
Plus embroidery (satin and stem stitch)
The Oakleigh Garden District is one of Mobile's (Alabama) three historic districts. It is nationally registered and represents a late 19th-century in-town residential area of approximately 500 homes. The ten houses I did in this series are still standing, and they look exactly as they are sewn. Before sewing each house, I began by photographing it on black and white film. While on site I also took notes and made small sketches for future reference. From the photos I then made a 30-

by-24-inch line drawing which became my master pattern. The completed houses were mounted over canvas stretcher bars and a custom frame was added.

Wisconsin Calf
Pillow
13 by 13 inches
Plus embroidery (satin and running stitches, and French knots)

Calico Stove
Pillow
14 by 8 inches
Plus embroidery (stem and satin stitch)

Rooster Weather Vane
Place mat (18 by 12 inches), table runner (42 by 14 inches), chair cushion (16½ by 15 inches), tea cozy (12½ by 10 inches), and wall hanging (15 by 16 inches)
Most people think of art projects in terms of one item. Typically, they move from one unrelated piece of needlecraft to another. But when you shop in retail department stores, most of the merchandise is coordinated. A coordinated theme has several items that are related by color, fabric, and subject matter. In this kitchen theme I wanted you to see several articles related by one sewing technique and one motif. Notice also that some of the larger items have elements that are added to them while smaller items have things that are subtracted.

1123 Palmetto Street
Wall Hanging
30 by 24 inches
Plus embroidery (satin and stem stitch)
Another hanging in my historic homes series. This way of recording a home makes a lovely anniversary present.

Calico Rooster
Wall Hanging
21 by 16 inches
First seen in *Country Handcrafts Bazaar*, 1983.

Calico Swan
Place Mat
18 by 12 inches

Tulips
Place Mat
18 by 12 inches

Angels
Christmas Tree Skirt
49-inch circle
First seen in *Country Handcrafts*, Autumn 1983.

Flower Girl Basket
Basket
5 by 8 inches
Cotton blends and polyester satin
Commercial pattern plus embroidery (satin, running, and French knots)
Appliqué can be applied to flat sections and then worked into a three-dimensional shape, which has a skeleton of cardboard, batting, and tape or some arrangement of wire, stuffing, and string.
First seen in *Needlecraft for Today*, May/June 1983.

Ring Bearer's Pillow
Pillow
10 by 10 inches
Cotton blends and polyester satin
Plus embroidery (French knots and single running stitch)
First seen in *Needlecraft for Today*, May/June 1983.

Amaryllis
Wall Hanging
17 by 29 inches
Plus embroidery (satin, chain, laced running, back, and trellis couching stitch)

Spring Bouquet
Wall Hanging
14 by 14 inches
Machine appliqué with seams plus embroidery (French knots, single running, satin, and backstitch) and quilting (diamond pattern)
This square hangs on the wall by two round plastic rings that are stitched to the top back side.

Tropical Fish (on cover)

Front Side of a Two-sided Banner
65 by 54 inches
Plus quilting (echo pattern)

Geisha (on cover)

Quilted Woman's Jacket
Plus embroidery (satin, cross, running, back, and stem stitch), quilting (parallel-line pattern), trapunto, machine-straight-stitching, braids, and tapes

Before work on the *geisha* ever began, I created my own quilted fabric by sandwiching one layer of batting between two layers of printed cotton. I then machine-straight-stitched parallel lines to hold the layers together. As the various parts of the woman were appliquéd to this heavy background, I stuffed the head, hands, and headdress from the top side. The embroidery was added after all the appliquéing and stuffing were complete. Unlike the lady's body, the parasol has no stuffing. Most of the decoration is created by the bias tapes and braids which were straight-stitched in position.

TECHNIQUES

In the machine appliqué-without-seams method, each appliqué shape is cut to the finished size. The raw edges are left flat and covered by a machine satin-stitch. This does not mean that there are no lapover areas, just that there are no seam allowances on the individual pattern pieces. Since this is the simplest and quickest method of appliqué, it can be used to decorate pillows, clothing, accessories, wall hangings, banners, and all sorts of items, which range from simple to complex. Use it as the only technique or mix it with embroidery, quilting, trapunto, beading, and all kinds of trims.

In most projects using this method (corduroy, denim, and sturdy upholstery fabrics of good weight are some of the exceptions), the background fabric is backed with a single layer of polyester traditional needle-punched batting before any appliquéing begins. This batting is essential because it adds weight to the supporting fabric, and it makes it easier to produce a nice flat satin stitch. To add the batting to the

Illus. 30. Master pattern.

Illus. 31. Background fabric.

3" Seam Allowances

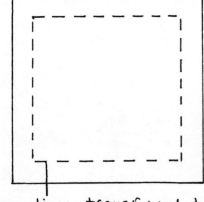

seam lines transferred to right side fabric

background fabric, follow this basic procedure as illustrated on a wall hanging (Illus. 30):

1. Lay out and cut your background fabric. Before the pattern is un-pinned, transfer the seam lines to the right side of this fabric with the lightest possible color of dressmaker's tracing paper and a tracing wheel (Illus. 31).

2. With the background pattern as your guide, lay out and cut one sheet of batting (Illus. 32).

Illus. 32. Batting.

3. With right sides up, pin the background fabric over the batting. Hand-baste the two layers together. Use a knotted double strand of regular thread and big running stitches. To avoid lumps and puckers, baste so that it is like the rays of the sun from the center of the shape to the outside edges. On large wall hangings which have a 3″ seam allowance, also baste close to the outside edge of the fabric (Illus. 33).

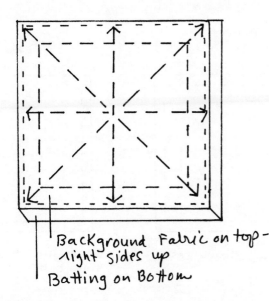

Illus. 33.

4. Sew over the seam line transferred to the right side of the background fabric. Use a single strand of bright-colored thread and ½″ running stitches. Sew through the batting also (Illus. 34). Use this stitched line on the cloth to register your master pattern and each part of the appliqué.

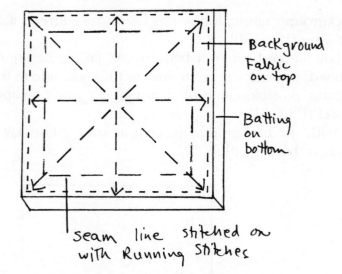

Illus. 34.

5. If your appliqué shapes have already been cut and marked, get ready to machine-appliqué. Refer to the general instructions which follow. See the sections "Registration" and "Machine-Satin-Stitching."

Machine Appliqué With Seams

In the machine appliqué-with-seams method, a ¼″ or ⅛″ seam allowance is added to each individual appliqué pattern. In addition, unlike machine appliqué without seams, the supporting fabric is never backed with batting, or the batting is added only after the appliqué is finished, say, for example, to combine appliqué and quilting. In this method the following basic procedure is used as illustrated on a place mat (Illus. 35):

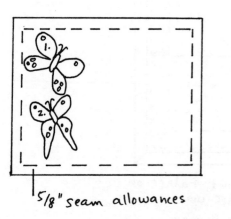

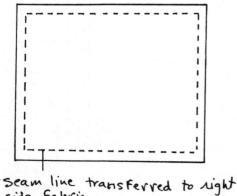

Illus. 35 (left). Master pattern.

Illus. 36 (right). Background fabric.

1. Lay out and cut the background fabric. Before the pattern is unpinned, transfer the seam lines to the right side of the fabric with the lightest color of dressmaker's tracing paper and a tracing wheel (Illus. 36).

2. Sew over the seam line transferred to the right side of the back-

ground fabric. Use a single strand of bright-colored thread and ½″ running stitches. Use this stitched line to register your master pattern and each part of the appliqué.

3. If it has not already been done, lay out and cut the appliqué shapes. Before the patterns are unpinned, transfer the seam lines and any inner markings to the right side of each fabric. Use pencil and the lightest possible color of dressmaker's tracing paper (Illus. 37).

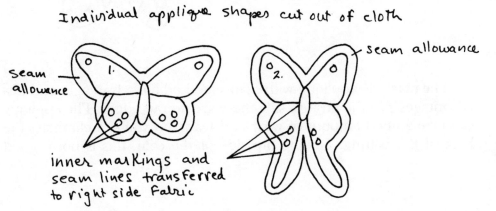

Individual applique shapes cut out of cloth

seam allowance

seam allowance

seam allowance

inner markings and seam lines transferred to right side Fabric

Illus. 37. Individual appliqué shapes cut out of cloth.

4. Machine-straight-stitch on the seam line of each individual appliqué. Use a matching thread (Illus. 38). *Note*: Use the same matching thread for the machine straight-stitching, the hand-tacking, and the machine satin-stitching.

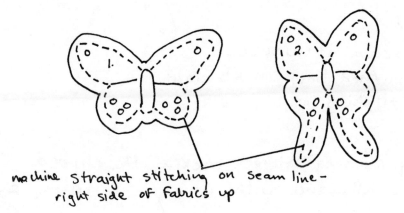

machine straight stitching on seam line – right side of Fabrics up

Illus. 38.

5. Clip, as needed, the curves and corners to the seam line (Illus. 39).
6. Fold back the clipped seam allowance. With a single strand of regular thread, tack the seam allowance to the wrong side of the shape with tiny running stitches positioned close to the folded edge (Illus. 40). These stitches will be hidden by the machine satin-stitching and are never removed.
7. Get ready to machine-appliqué. Refer to the general instructions, which follow. See "Registration" and "Machine-Satin-Stitching."

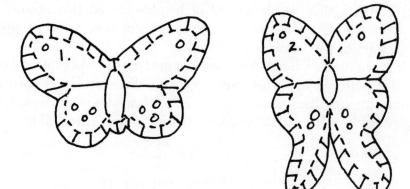

Illus. 39. Seam allowances clipped to machine-straight-stitching lines.

The machine appliqué-with-seams method has advantages and disadvantages. On the positive side there are no raw edges. The appliqué can take a good amount of wear and tear, and you can eliminate the bulk of the batting. On the flip side of the coin, this is not a good

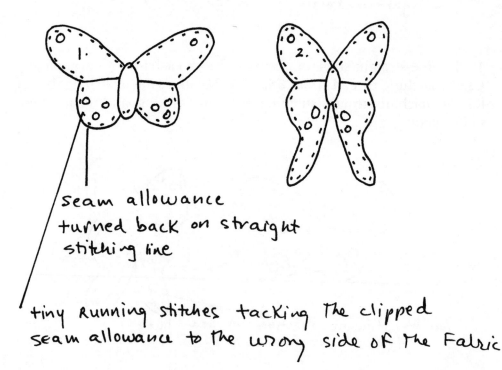

seam allowance
turned back on straight
stitching line

Illus. 40.

tiny Running stitches tacking The clipped
seam allowance to the wrong side of the Fabric

technique for a design that involves a lot of layering in concentrated areas. Because of the double thickness of fabric at the edge of each individual shape, the satin-stitching builds up. After two or three layers, mounds of satin-stitching form at the corners and other pivoting points. To eliminate this problem select designs which have spread-out shapes and just a few tiers of fabric.

Registration

Once you have gone through the effort of making a full-size drawing and positioning it in just the right place on the master pattern, it is important not to alter the look of the design. Registration, i.e., the exact matching of lines and shapes on the supporting cloth with the corresponding lines and shapes on the master pattern, will provide this exact placement of the appliqué. To register each part of your appliqué, follow these steps:

1. With right sides up place your master pattern over the background fabric.

2. Line up the seam lines on the master pattern with the seam lines stitched on the cloth. Do not get into the habit of registering the master pattern by lining up the edges in the paper with the edges in the cloth. The cloth will be unravelling and shrinking as you sew, and your registration will not be true.

3. When the seam lines in paper match the seam lines in cloth, pin the master pattern to the fabric in the top seam allowance (Illus. 41).

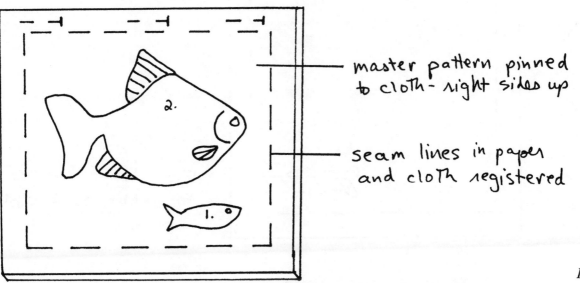

master pattern pinned to cloth - right sides up

seam lines in paper and cloth registered

Illus. 41.

4. Lift up the bottom of the master pattern and slip appliqué #1 (right sides up) onto the background. Move the cloth shape until the edges of the fabric match the edges in the master pattern. At that point the shape is registered (Illus. 42).

5. Pin the appliqué in place. Remove the master pattern. Hand-baste the appliqué to the background with big running stitches (Illus. 43).

6. Although the next step is to machine-satin-stitch once around the shape, continue this process of registering the master pattern, registering the shape, pinning, basting, sewing, and pressing until the entire design has been finished.

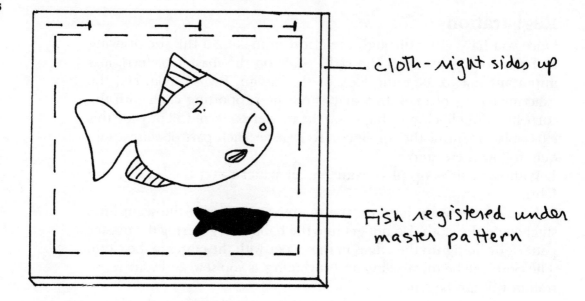

Illus. 42.

cloth - right sides up

Fish registered under master pattern

Illus. 43.

Fish hand basted to background cloth

Machine-Satin-Stitching

As soon as each appliqué is registered and hand-basted to the background, it is ready for satin-stitching. Add the satin-stitch foot to your machine and thread up the top of the machine with a matching thread. For the bobbin it is not necessary to match or change the thread with such frequency. I normally use a white or beige bobbin to harmonize with all the light-colored threads and a black or brown bobbin for all the dark. If you are a beginner, having the same color top and bottom threads has its advantages. For example, if the bobbin thread happens to appear on the top side of the fabric, it does not matter.

When you are ready to satin-stitch once around the outside edge of the appliqué, you will have to select your stitch width. The width of your stitching depends on the weight of the fabric and the degree it unravels. On my machine the stitch-width control is a dial with numbers 1 through 4. The higher the number, the wider the stitch. On lightweight and medium fabrics, I usually select a setting of 2½ (about ³⁄₁₆″ wide). On heavy fabrics like corduroy or denim, a setting of 3 or 3¼ (about ¼″) works well.

The top tension control is another dial on your machine that is important in appliqué. Usually, whenever you satin-stitch, the top thread tension is loosened slightly. Also, the wider the stitch, the looser the tension. Test your stitching on a scrap of the fabric under consideration, and readjust your tension for different weights of fabrics, the thickness of the layers, the width of the stitch, and even the size of the spool. Check your sewing-machine manual for the correct way to reset your tension.

With machine appliqué it is important that the placement of the stitching should be exact. Learn to get the outer edge of the stitching right on the edge of the shape (Illus. 44–46). Keep in mind also that on

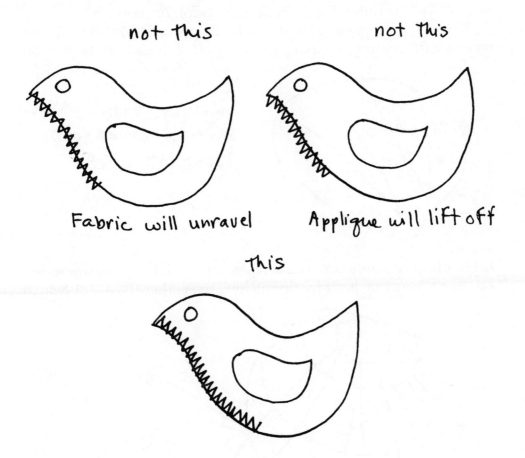

Illus. 44–46.

corners and curves, the needle is left in the fabric. Make your machine adjustments by lifting up the presser foot, pivoting or turning (Illus. 47), and then lowering the presser foot. As you continue stitching, you will overlap some of the previous stitches. When you have finished sewing, knot all threads on the reverse side and cut off the excess.

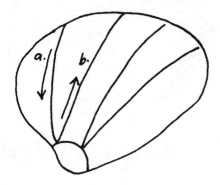

satin Stitch
Foot is up,
but needle is
still in Fabric

Illus. 47.

In machine appliqué the inner lines are stitched only after the entire shape has been secured. For interest, these inner lines can vary in their width and in the number of times they are sewn. Make them 1/16", 1/8", 3/16", or wider. Stitch them once, twice, or more.

If you have a great deal of machine appliqué, you will want to minimize the starting, stopping, and tying off of threads. So before you

machine satin stitch in direction of arrows. Pivot at point

Illus. 48. Machine-satin-stitch in direction of arrows. Pivot at point.

begin stitching, study your master pattern. Look for areas where you can move from one line of satin-stitching to another (Illus. 48). Search

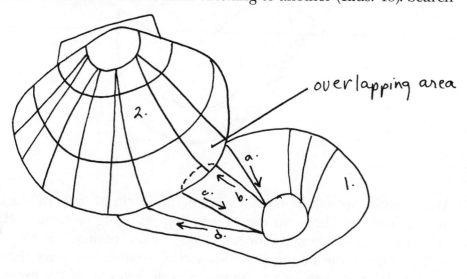

overlapping area

Illus. 49. Machine-satin-stitch in direction of arrows. Broken lines are travelling stitches.

out areas that you can travel across because they will be overlapped by another part of the design (Illus. 49). Make use of the seam allowances as pickup points for other lines (Illus. 50). If you want these travelling stitches to be very inconspicuous, end one line of satin-stitching, switch to a straight stitch in the travelling areas, and resume the satin-stitching when you have reached the new starting point (Illus. 51).

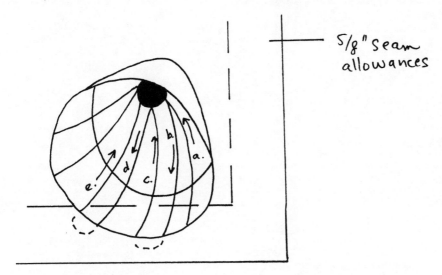

5/8" seam allowances

Illus. 50. Machine-satin-stitch in direction of arrows. Broken lines are travelling stitches.

Pressing is an absolutely essential part of machine appliqué. Each time a shape is sewn on the background, it must be pressed smooth and flat. This step is simple but a crucial part in achieving a wrinkle-free design.

—— Satin Stitching

—— machine straight stitching in the travelling area

—— satin stitching resumed

Illus. 51.

COMBINING TECHNIQUES

When you have finished doing the machine appliqué, there are other needlecraft techniques which mix well with appliqué. Consider, for example, appliqué plus embroidery, quilting, or trapunto.

Appliqué Plus Embroidery

On many occasions there are areas in the design that are too small or too complicated to machine-satin-stitch, but the details are essential to complete the total look of the design. At other times, you may be looking for a fabric that has a specific pattern and it cannot be found. Or maybe you need to add some tiny touches of texture and variety to make the work uniquely yours. In all these instances think about combining appliqué and hand-embroidery. Use the appliqué for the large broad areas; use the embroidery for the small fine details.

The choice of the embroidery stitches depends on the design, but any of the following are compatible. Try, for example, the satin, cross, chain, buttonhole, feather, stem, roumanian, trellis-couching, back, running, and french knots (Illus. 52–62).

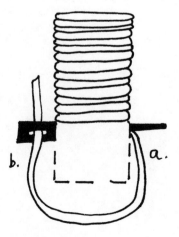

Illus. 52. Satin stitch.

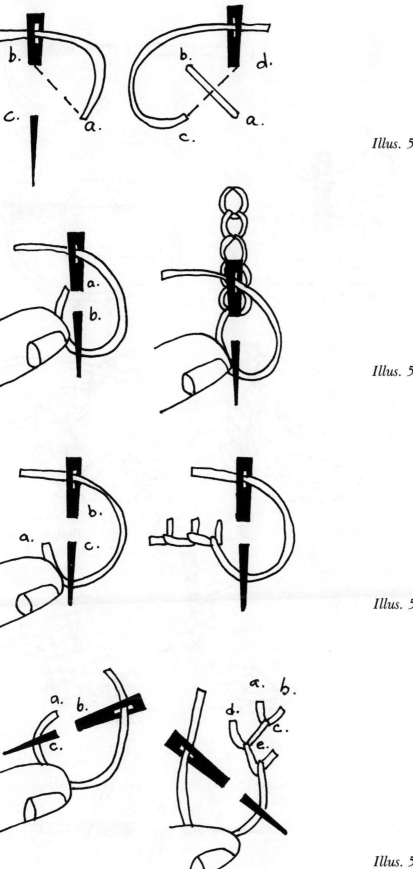

Illus. 53. Cross.

Illus. 54. Chain.

Illus. 55. Buttonhole.

Illus. 56. Feather.

Illus. 57. Stem.

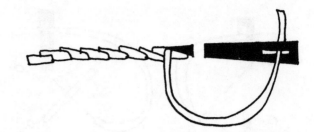

Illus. 58. Roumanian.

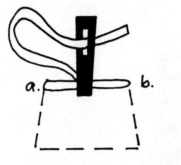

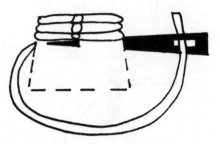

Illus. 59. Trellis couching.

the tying stitch can be either this <u>OR</u> this—a full cross

Illus. 60. Back.

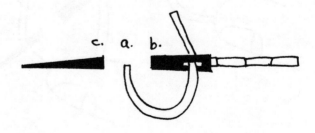

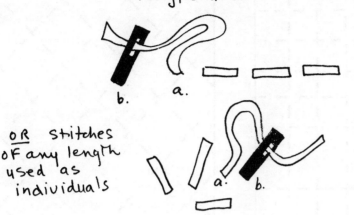

Running-stitches of equal length used in a line

OR stitches of any length used as individuals

Illus. 61.

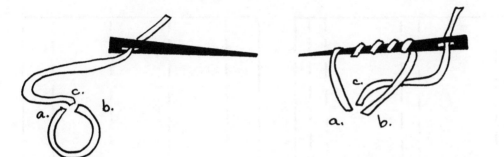

Illus. 62. French knots.

When you are ready to execute the embroidery, you can either transfer the design to the right side of the fabric with pencil and dressmaker's tracing paper or judge and sew it freehand. Divide the six separate strands of floss into groups of two or three threads and use a crewel needle.

Using the Proper Embroidery Tools

Needles. Choose a size 7 or 8 crewel/embroidery needle.
Threads. Use either the J. & P. Coats deluxe six-strand floss or DMC's six-strand (mouliné special). As a word of caution, watch out for the DMC reds, blues, and oranges. These colors can bleed and stain light surrounding areas. Before a stitch is taken, rinse these threads several times in water until all traces of the color disappear. Then dip the skein in a bath of water and one teaspoon of white vinegar. Blot off the excess water and let dry.

Appliqué plus Quilting

In a machine-appliquéd design, quilting is usually used to fill plain, large open areas and to prevent several layers of fabric from shifting, puckering, and bunching. These tiny even running stitches also add decoration, texture, and strength to the surface in a variety of patterns (Illus. 63–71).

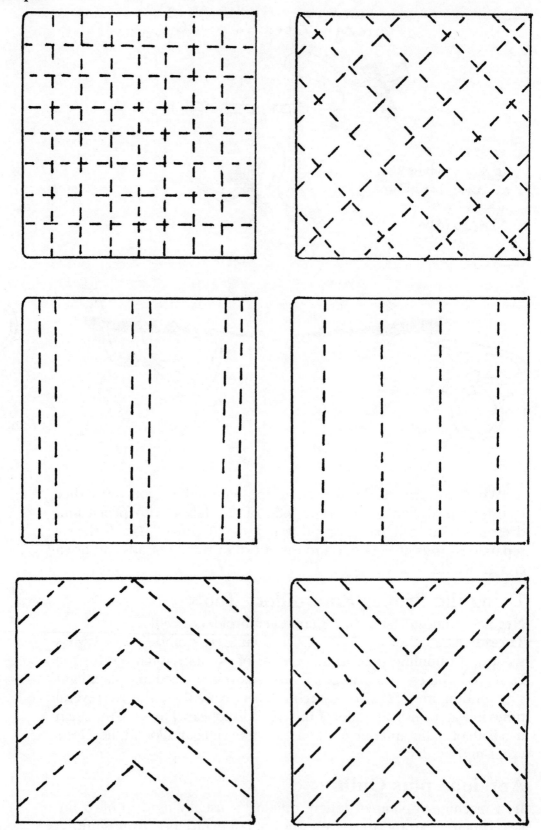

Illus. 63–68. Quilting patterns.

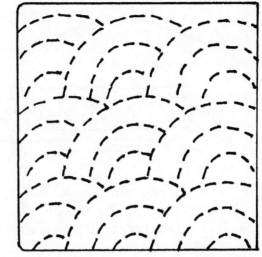

Illus. 69–70. More quilting patterns.

Illus. 71. Echo quilting—quilt ¼" away from edge of shape(s).

Quilted articles are made of three layers: the decorated top, the polyester batting, and the protective backing. The quilting stitch, made with a single strand of thread, goes through all the layers.

To quilt, use a quilting needle, a matching quilting thread, and a thimble. Frames and hoops are optional. After the three layers are assembled and hand-basted from the center to the outer edges, mark your quilting pattern on the right side of the top fabric. Use a clear plastic ruler or templates with either a fine-point water-soluble pen, a #2 pencil, a white pencil, or a washable cloth marker. Test your markers on a scrap fabric to make sure they do wash out.

Begin quilting with a single strand of 16-inch thread. Make a small knot at the end. From the backing, come up to where you want to start quilting. Gently pull the knot through the backing til it gets buried in the batting. Pull the needle out and start quilting with two or three small even running stitches that pass through all the layers (Illus. 72). Continue making tiny stitches that are uniform in size and spacing.

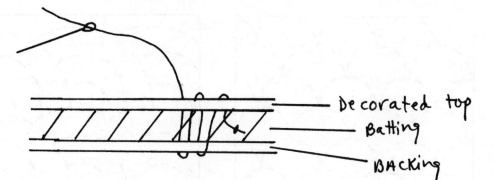

Illus. 72.

To end your thread, make two small knots close to the quilt top. Run your needle through the batting and out to the quilt top. Once again the knots will be buried in the batting. Clip the thread close to the quilt surface.

Using the Proper Quilting Tools

Needles. Choose a size 7, 8, or 9 needle, sometimes called a between. A between is a short narrow needle with a round eye and a sharp point that is easier to control than the typical long needle.

Threads. Most quilters prefer to use a quilting thread of 100% cotton, but there is a spool of cotton-covered polyester with Extra Strong Hand Quilting on the label. Although quilting threads come in a limited range of colors, your thread color should match the predominant color in the quilt top. As a result, irregularities in stitch size and spacing will not be so noticeable.

Polyester Batting in Combination With Quilting. Polyester traditional needle-punched batting is available in seamless sheets of various sizes (crib—45″×60″, twin—72″×90″, full—81″×96″, and queen—90″×108″). It is nonallergenic, washable, and cuts like a fabric.

Appliqué plus Trapunto (Stuffing)

Machine appliqué can have a three-dimensional appearance, i.e., a sculptural effect, when individual shapes are stuffed with small amounts of 100%-pure polyester fibre. This material is sold in packages of 12 or 24 ounces, and the fibres are nonallergenic, hand-washable, and easy to pull apart. The stuffing can be added by working from either the top or the back of the design. The methods are as follows:

Illus. 73. Background fabric—right sides up.

1. *Stuffing from the top.* Machine-appliqué as usual but stitch around only three quarters of the shape to be stuffed. Push the fibrefill inside through the opening (Illus. 73). Distribute it evenly. Hand-baste the open area closed before machine-satin-stitching the remainder of the shape (Illus. 74).

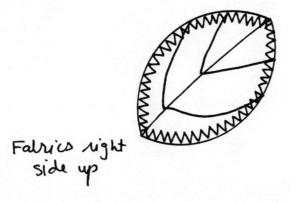

Fabrics right side up

Illus. 74. Fabrics right side up.

2. *Stuffing from the back.* Before any machine-appliquéing is done, add a backing to the supporting fabric (wrong sides together). Baste the two layers together and machine-appliqué as usual. From the wrong side of the design, make one or several small slits in the backing within the

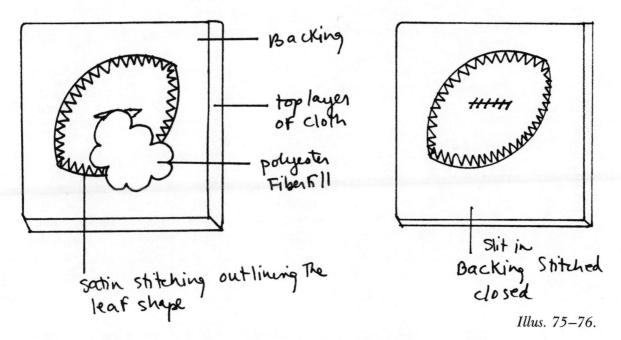

Backing

top layer of cloth

polyester Fiberfill

satin stitching outlining the leaf shape

Slit in Backing Stitched closed

Illus. 75–76.

area enclosed by the machine satin-stitching (Illus. 75). Be careful not to cut through to the appliqué. Insert bits of stuffing through the holes and do not overstuff. Close the holes by butting the edges of the fabric together and slipstitching (Illus. 76).

BITS AND PIECES

Protect your textile designs from light, dust, insects, rodents, and mildew. Do not hang them in direct sunlight, in fluorescent lighting, or near heat and ventilation ducts. Framed textiles should not be covered with glass. Let the fabrics breathe and allow the air to circulate on them. The dust that accumulates on framed or hanging examples can be removed by gentle brushing, dusting, or vacuuming.

If fabrics must be stored, store them flat or rolled with tissue paper placed within the rolls. Line wooden drawers or paper boxes with acid-free paper or washed, unbleached muslin, and keep the fabrics away from staples, nails, and pins. Clear plastic boxes are also good for storage, but do not use plastic bags of any kind.

Mounting Textiles over Stretcher Bars

Artist's canvas stretcher bars are pieces of wood that interlock to form either a square or rectangle. Two are needed for the length and two are needed for the width. They can be purchased in art, frame, and hobby shops in sizes from 5″ to 50″. Fredrix and Anco Bilt are two of the more common brands of stretchers.

Once you have decided to mount your appliqué on artist's canvas stretcher bars, follow these steps:

1. Press and cut a *backing* from a medium-weight cotton. Cut the *backing* the same size as the decorated *front*, seam allowances included.

2. With wrong sides together lay the *front* over the *backing*. Smooth out the layers. Pin them together (Illus. 77).

3. Place the *front/back* combination face down on a flat surface. Place the stretcher bars over the *backing* and center the wood (Illus. 78).

4. Stretch each side of the wall hanging over the stretcher bars. Start by temporarily placing one tack in the center of each side (Illus. 79). Turn the *front* over to see if it is properly centered.

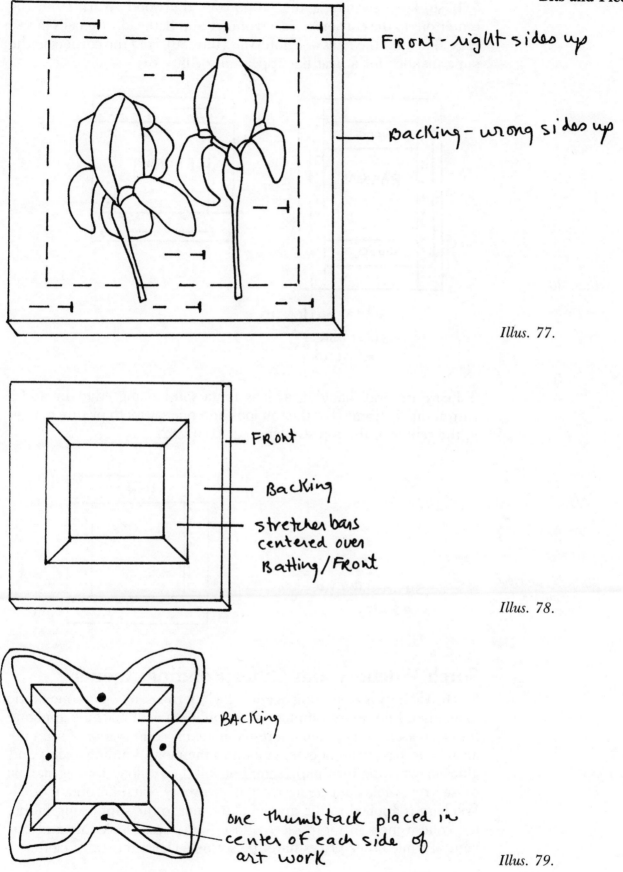

FROnt - right sides up

Backing - wrong sides up

Illus. 77.

FROnt

Backing

stretcher bars
centered over
Batting/FROnt

Illus. 78.

BACKing

one thumbtack placed in
center of each side of
art work

Illus. 79.

5. If so, keep stretching the fabric over the wood. Work from the center out to the corners. Use a hammer and flathead wire nails in size ½ × 19. Insert the nails at 1″ intervals (Illus 80). Fold the corners in the same manner for a neat flat appearance (Illus. 81).

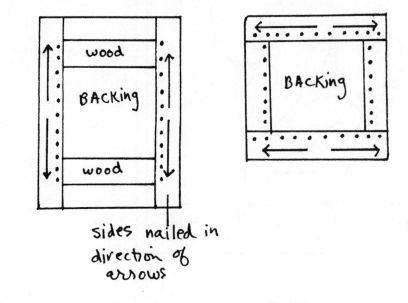

Illus. 80–81.

6. Leave the wall hanging as it is for a soft-looking edge, or add a custom-made frame. For the soft look add one sawtooth picture hanger in the center of the top stretcher bar (Illus. 82).

Illus. 82. Sawtooth hanger added.

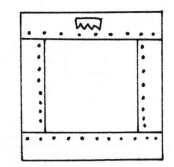

Stitch Witchery and Other Bonding Agents

Stitch Witchery is a bonding agent, which permanently joins one fabric to another. I do not recommend that you use it with machine appliqué for two reasons. First, I am interested in textile conservation. I want my artwork to pass from one generation to the next. Bonding agents and glues may be fine for the present, but will they yellow, disintegrate, or cause irreversible damage in five, ten, or twenty years? Second, if Stitch Witchery is applied to the appliqué and not to the supporting fabric, the cohesiveness in the project is lost. Some areas look stiff and unnatural while other places have the softness characteristic of cloth.

Strengthening Tracing Paper

If, for example, you have finished doing the appliqué, and you are ready to transfer the areas to be embroidered to the right side of the fabric, put single strips of transparent tape over and around this area on the master pattern (Illus. 83). Then go ahead and draw on the lines in the master pattern. The tracing paper will not rip apart with this reinforcement.

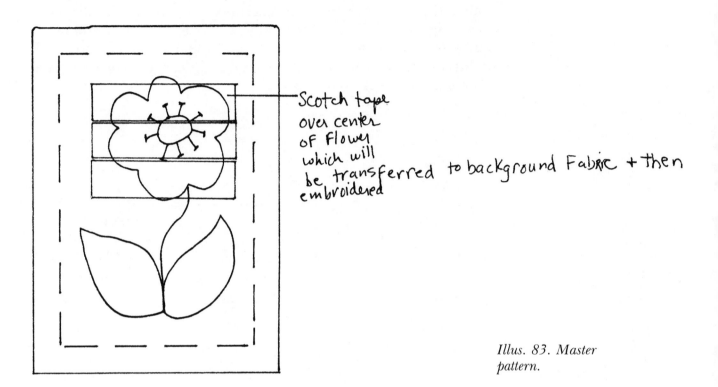

Scotch tape over center of flower which will be transferred to background fabric + then embroidered

Illus. 83. Master pattern.

Colors Showing Through on the Appliqué

If you do not want the bottom fabric to be seen through the top one, you can: 1. Double the top fabric and treat it as one; 2. Back the top fabric with a single layer of woven (not bonded) interfacing cut to size; or; 3. Place a piece of thin cotton flannel behind the appliqué.

Very Narrow Satin-Stitching

On very narrow satin-stitching, the bobbin thread may show through on the top side of the fabric even when you have tried all kinds of tension adjustment. In this instance go ahead and thread the bobbin with thread that matches the top of the machine.

Appliquéd Clothing

In general, avoid sewing in the areas with curves. Plan your designs so they do not cover the bust, hips, elbows, knees, rear end, and darts.

Removing Frayed Bits of Cloth

In the machine appliqué-without-seams method, frayed threads will pop up. To remove these individual threads, grab hold of each with tweezers. Then cut the thread close to the satin-stitching with sharp fine scissors.

Lapover Areas

Under normal circumstances each appliqué is satin-stitched once around the outside edge. The exception to this rule involves the lapover areas added to the appliqués. If, for example, you think the satin-stitching around the bottom shape would detract or create an unpleasant ridge in the top shape, you can do one of two things as illustrated on a duck (Illus. 85):

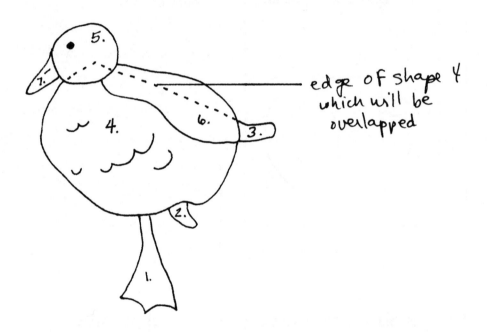

Illus. 84.

1. Machine-satin-stitch as usual once around the shape until you get to the lapover area. Do not sew this edge. Leave it plain (Illus. 85).

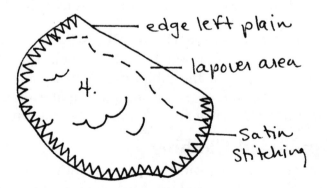

Illus. 85.

2. Machine-satin-stitch as usual once around the shape until you get to the lapover area. At this point switch to a machine straight-stitch; stitch that area only with a stitch ⅛" from the edge of the shape; then resume machine satin-stitching (Illus. 86).

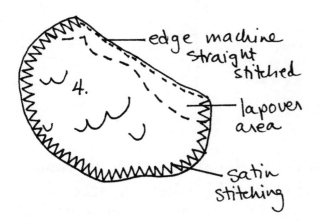

Illus. 86.

The Registration Line on the Supporting Fabric

Although I have always been emphatic about matching the seam lines on the master pattern with the lines stitched on the supporting fabric, this registration line will not always be true. On large projects, like my historic houses, all of the layering and machine-stitching caused the cloth to shrink about 1". To prepare for this eventuality, register off all four seam lines for as long as possible. Once the cloth starts to shrink, register off the top seam line and the sides (Illus. 87) or, at least, the top and one particular side (Illus. 88).

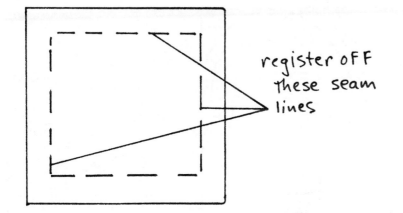

Illus. 87. Master pattern.

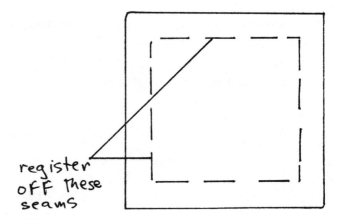

Illus. 88. Master pattern.

The Machine Appliqué Recap (or How to Get from a Line Drawing to a Finished Project)

Although this section explains the complete techniques of machine appliqué with and without seams, the patterns can usually be translated into fabric by following these thirteen steps:

1. Decide on a design, your color scheme, and the surface you will be decorating.

2. Preshrink and iron all fabrics.

3. With pencil, transfer the appliqué pattern to the center of a sheet of tracing paper (Illus. 89 and 90).

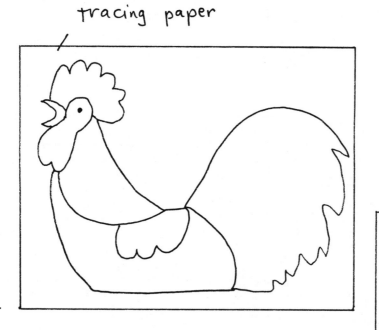

Illus. 89.

Illus. 90.

4. With pencil and tracing paper, draw the outline of the actual item or the part of the item that will carry the appliqué. On a commercial pattern or pattern of your own making, draw the edges of the article as well as the seam and cutting lines (Illus. 91). On wall hangings and

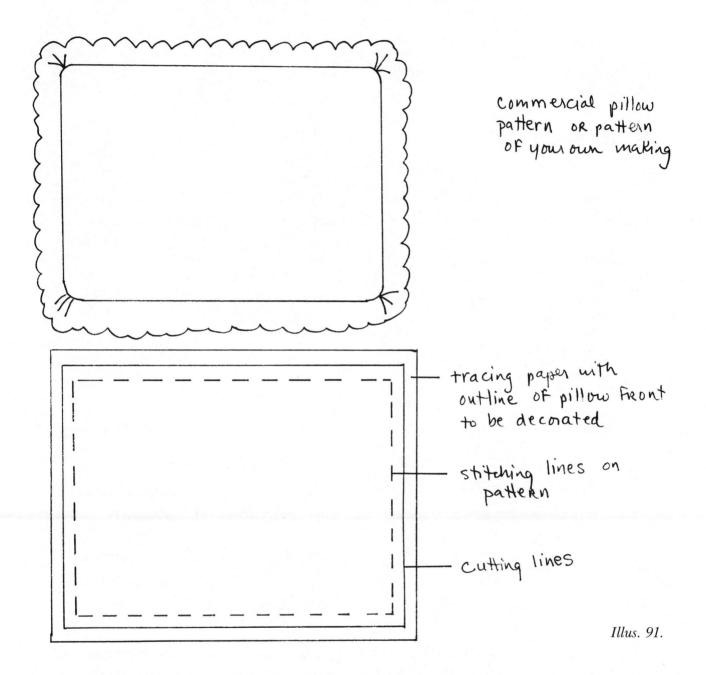

commercial pillow pattern or pattern of your own making

tracing paper with outline of pillow front to be decorated

stitching lines on pattern

cutting lines

Illus. 91.

banners, do not forget to add 3″ seam allowances beyond the actual edge of the article. On a ready-to-wear garment, draw the edges of the garment (Illus. 92).
5. With right sides up, put the tracing of the shape that is to carry the design over the pattern tracing. Slide the pattern tracing around to the

*Illus. 92. Child's ready-
to-wear garment.*

actual edge of garment

tracing paper with outline of
pinafore front that is to
be appliqued.

best possible position. Transfer the pattern to the supporting shape (Illus. 93 and 94). Use this tracing as your master pattern. (The master pattern is a kind of architectural blueprint which has several functions: It carries the full-size design in its proper position on the supporting shape; it is used to make the patterns for the individual appliqué shapes; and it is used to register each part of the appliqué in its correct position on the background.)

Illus. 93.

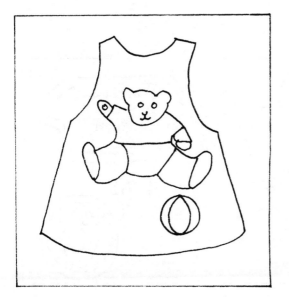

Illus. 94.

6. Decide on the order in which you will assemble your appliqué. Pencil your decisions onto the master pattern.

7. From your master pattern make the individual appliqué patterns. Use tracing paper and pencil. Add ¼ inch seam allowances if you are using the machine appliqué-with-seams method. Add any lapover areas (Illus. 95 and 96).

8. Lay out and cut the appliqué patterns. Before the patterns are un-pinned, transfer any inner markings to the right side of each fabric with the lightest possible color of dressmaker's tracing paper and pencil.

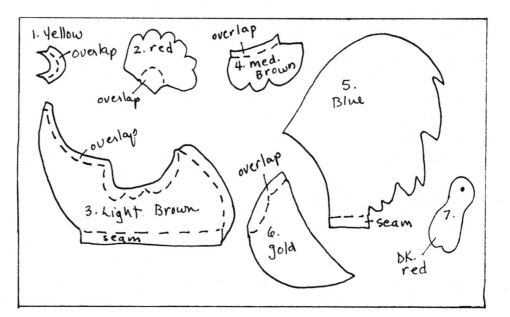

Illus. 95. Machine appliqué without seams.

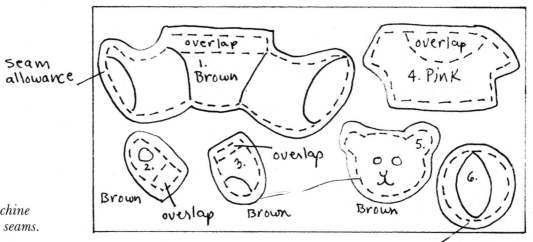

Illus. 96. Machine appliqué with seams.

9. On a commercial pattern or a project of your own making, lay out and cut the supporting background fabric and any batting being used. Before the pattern is unpinned, transfer the stitching lines to the right side of the fabric. Use the lightest possible color of dressmaker's tracing paper and a tracing wheel.

With right sides up, place the supporting fabric over the batting. Baste them together, and sew like rays of the sun.

Hand-sew over the transferred stitching lines so that they appear as ½" running stitches in a bright colored thread. Use this line to register your master pattern (Illus. 97).

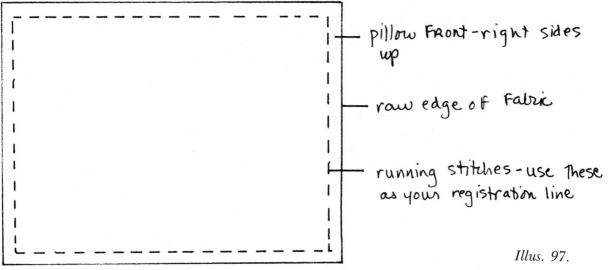

pillow Front - right sides up

raw edge of Fabric

running stitches - use These as your registration line

Illus. 97.

10. Start appliquéing. Register and pin your master pattern on the background fabric. On a ready-to-wear item, line up the edges pencilled on the tracing paper with the edges of the actual article. On a commercial pattern or project of your own design, line up the stitching lines pencilled on the tracing paper with the running stitches sewn on the front of the actual item. Register appliqué #1 under the master pattern. Pin. Hand-baste. Satin-stitch once around each shape with a 3/16″ width. Press. Stitch any inner lines only after the entire shape has been secured. Keep repeating this sequence of registering, pinning, hand-basting, satin-stitching, and pressing each part of the design until it is finished.

11. Add any touches of embroidery, quilting, or trapunto.

12. Finish off the article. Complete it, for instance, by just sewing the item together, mounting the design on canvas stretcher bars (if so, do not forget to wash it first), suspending the project from a pole, or adding circular rings to the top back edge.

13. Wash and iron the project.

THE PATTERNS

The line drawings in this section are machine-appliqué patterns (design ideas) that you can use to decorate clothing, accessories, and items for the home (pillows, bedding, tableware, wall hangings, and banners). The full-sized patterns can be used exactly as they are, combined with other drawings found in these pages, or mixed with artwork of your own. They can also be simplified, enriched, isolated, enlarged, or reduced in size. You can use them strictly for machine appliqué or combine them with embroidery, quilting, and trapunto.

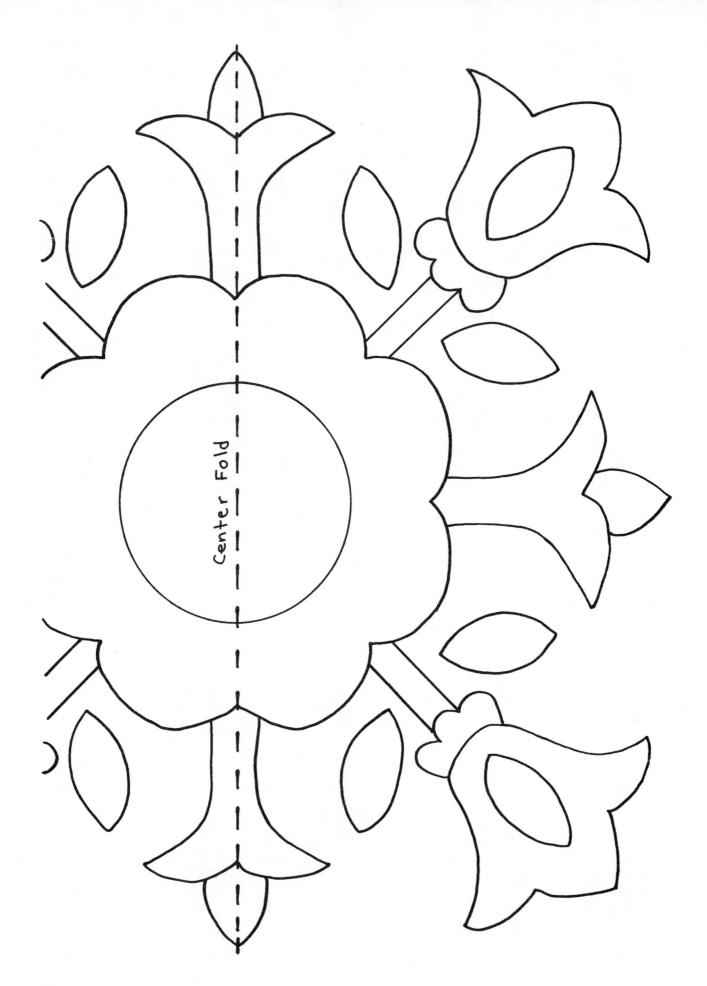

Center Fold

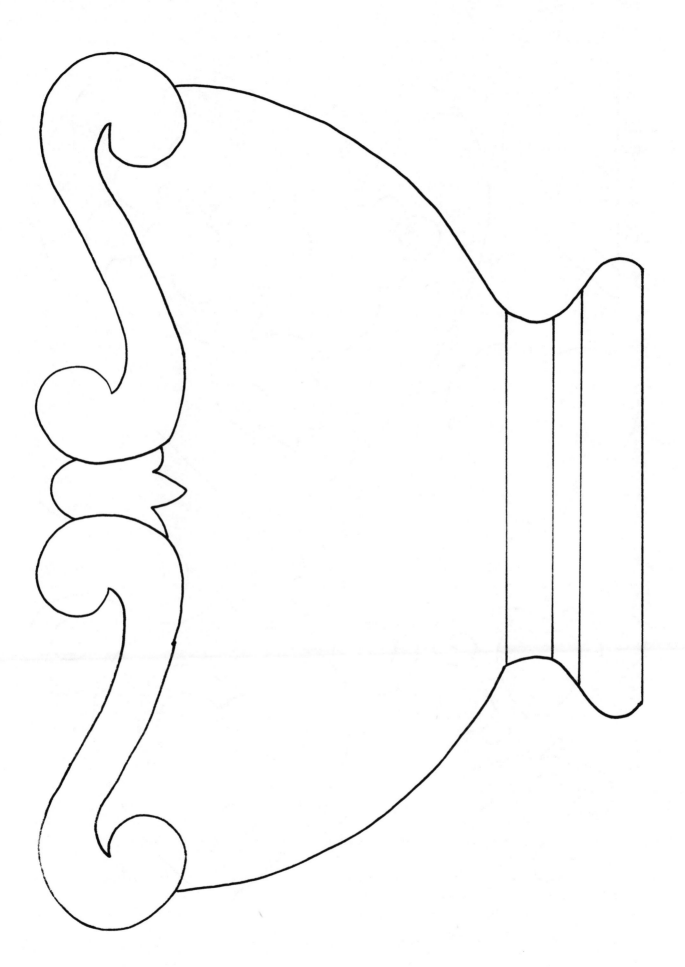

Center Fold

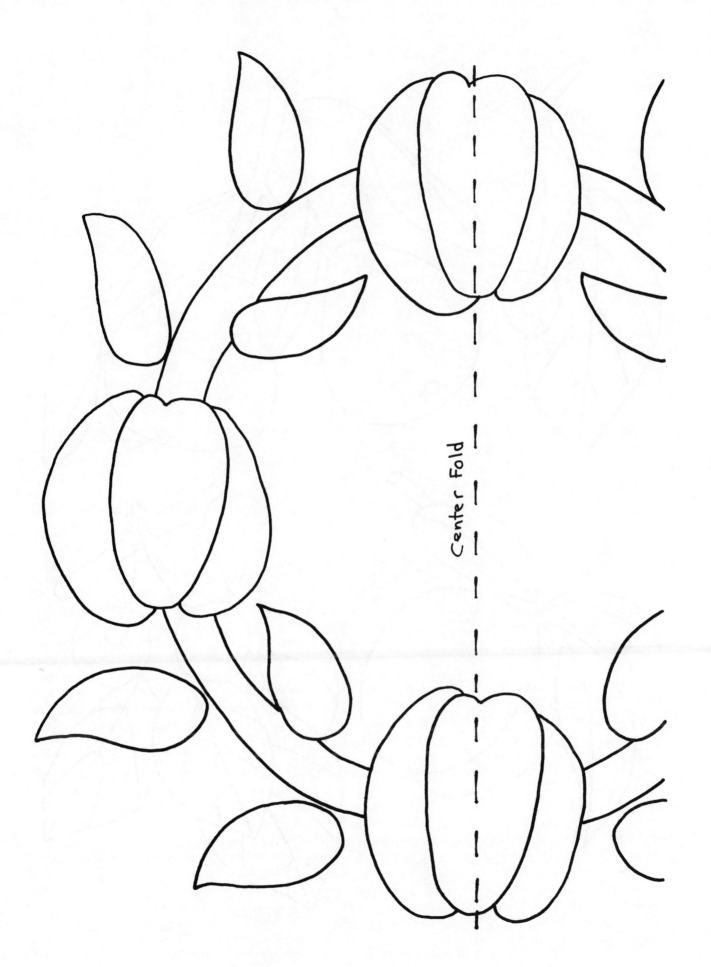

Center Fold

101

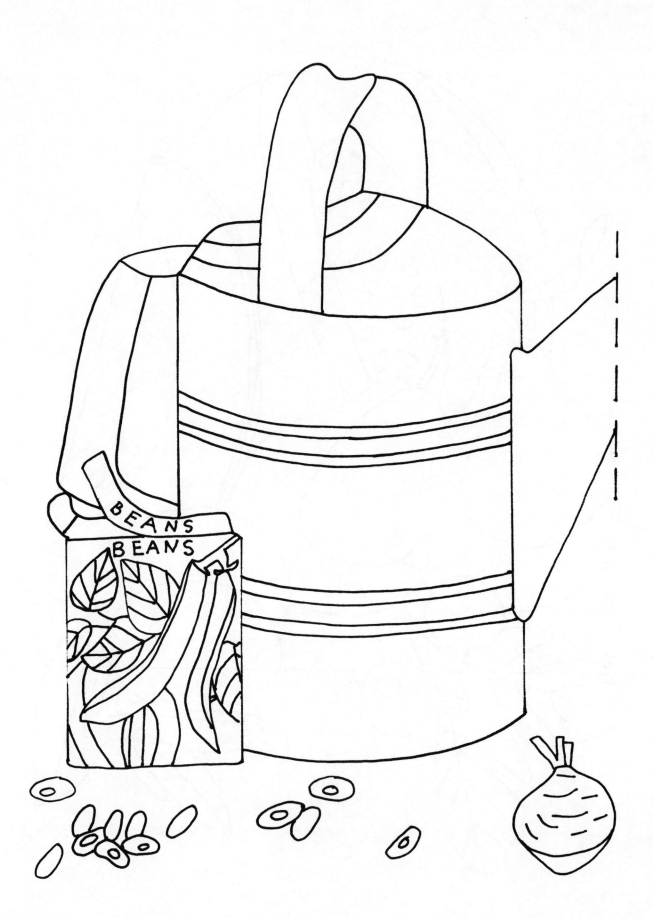

End of
Watering Can

ONION

RADISH

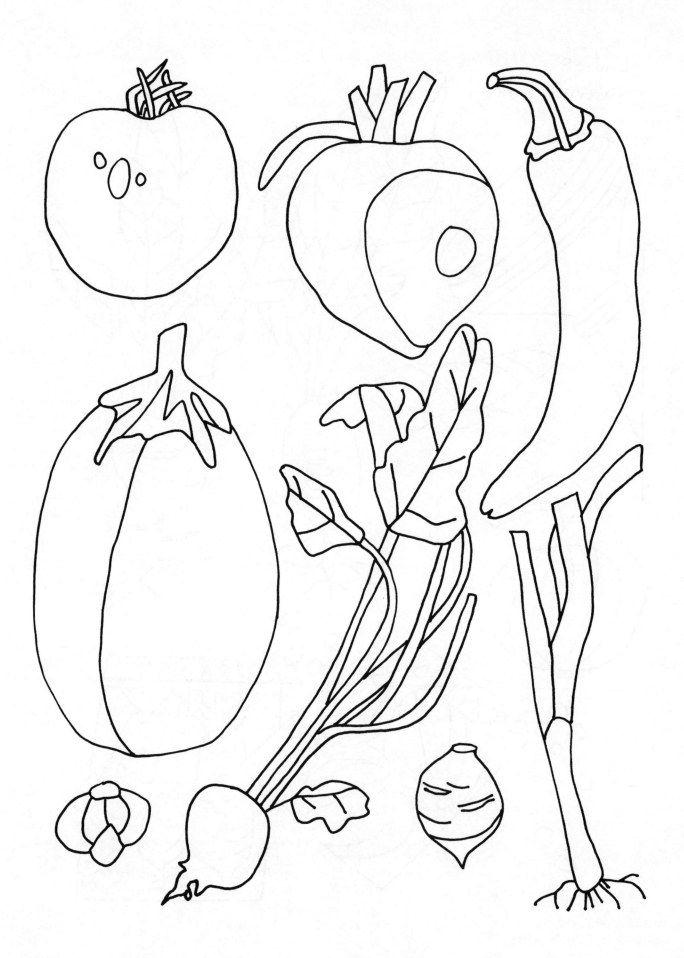

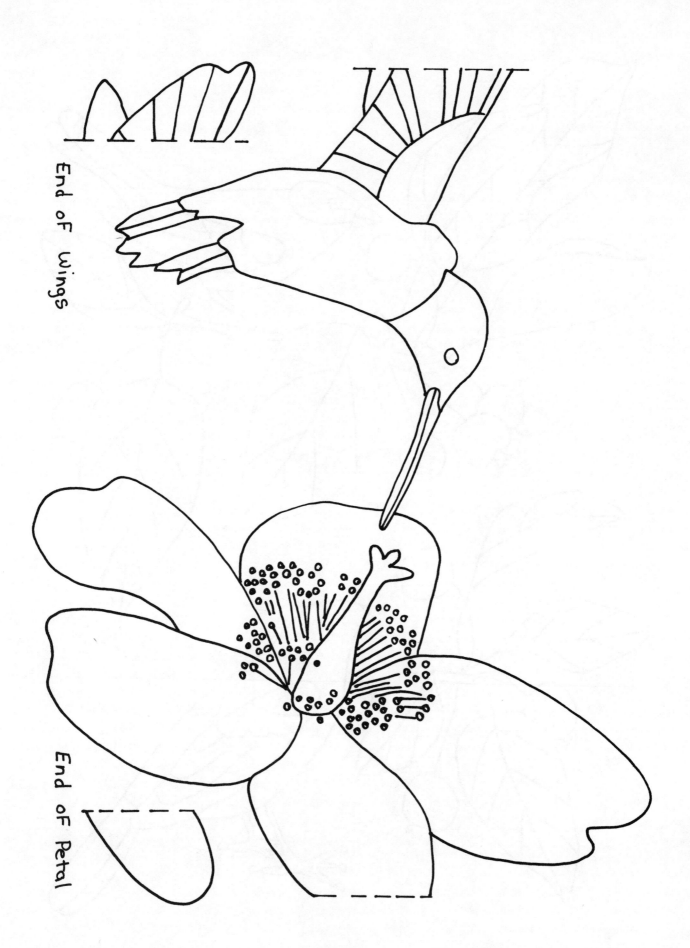

End of Wings

End of Petal

108

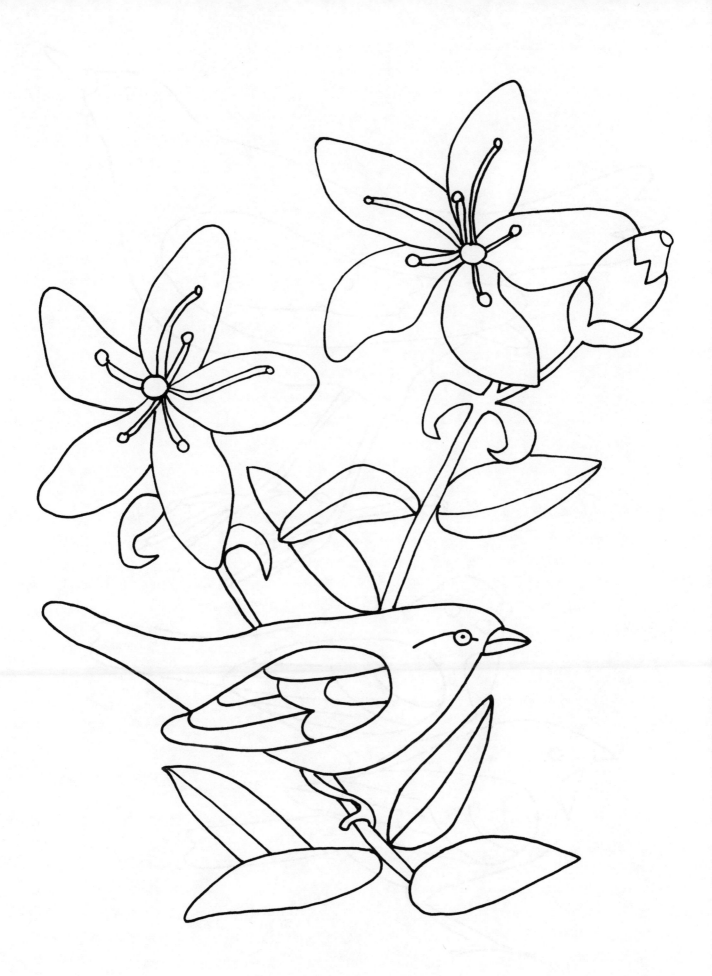

113

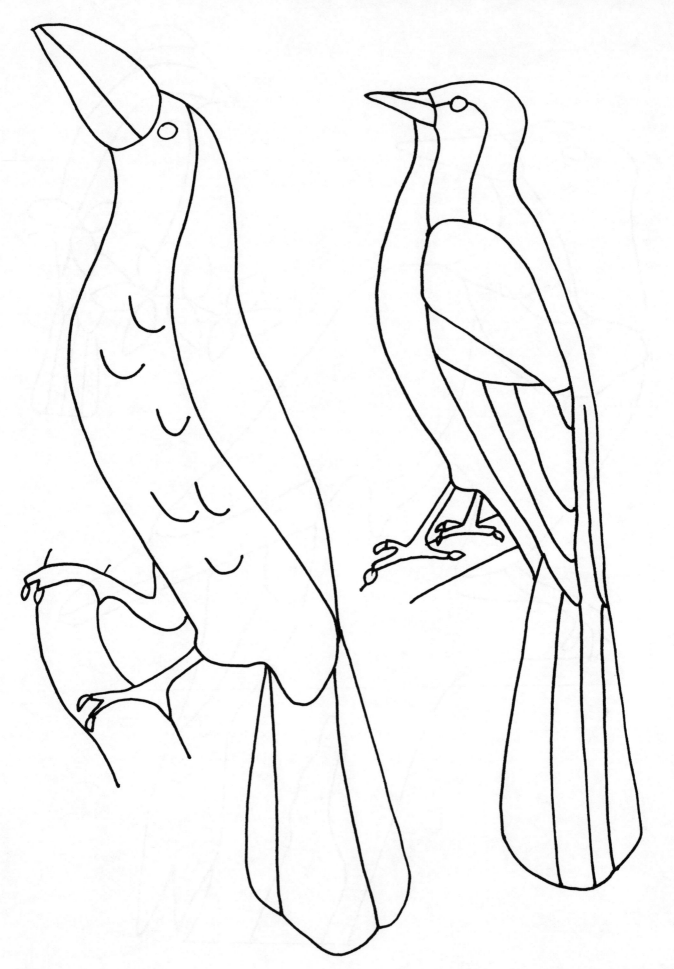

114

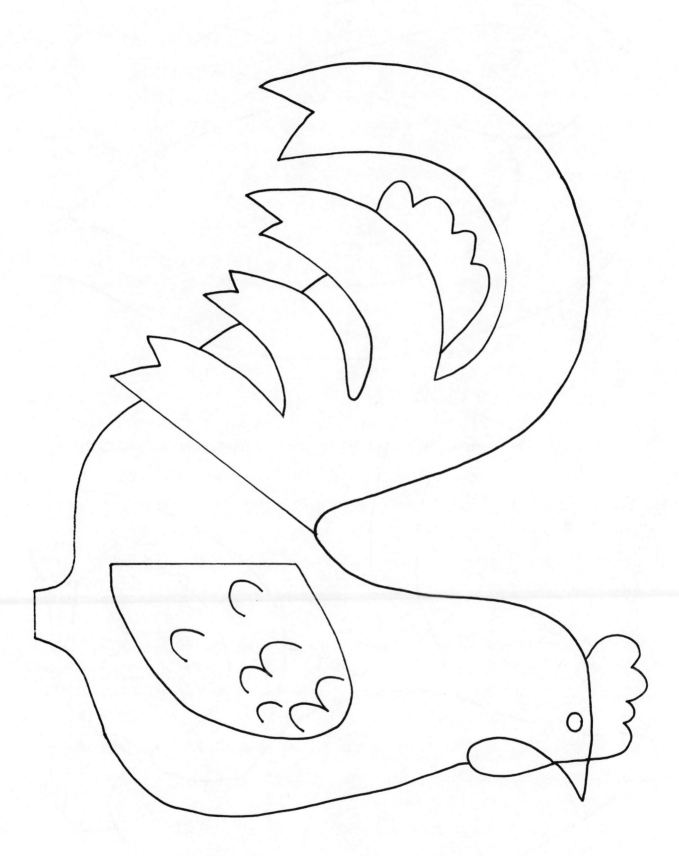

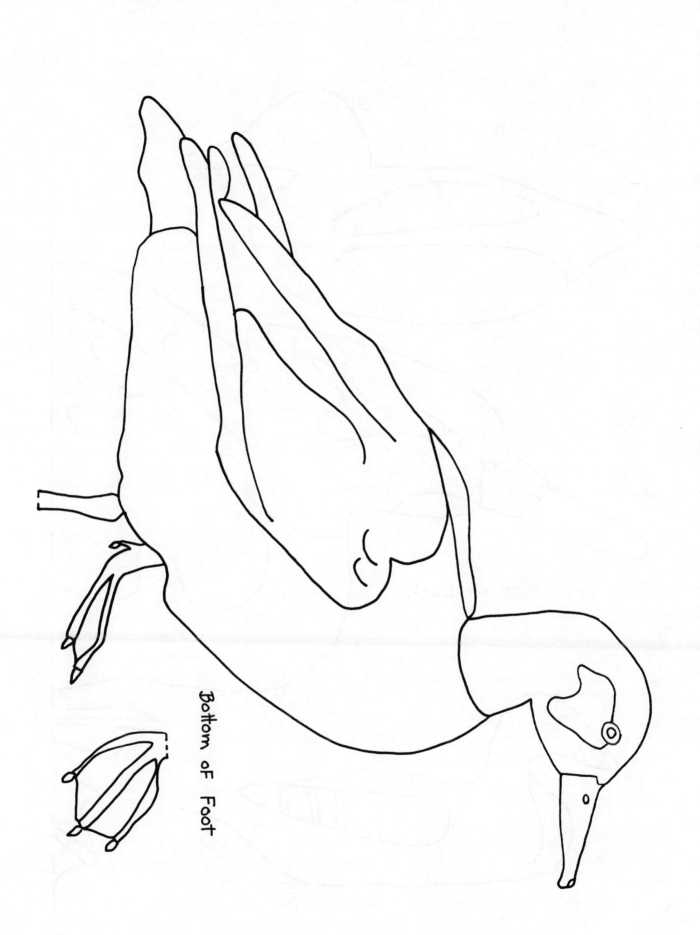

Bottom of Foot

117

Left side of Duck

Right side of Duck

Left side of Swan

120

Right side of Swan

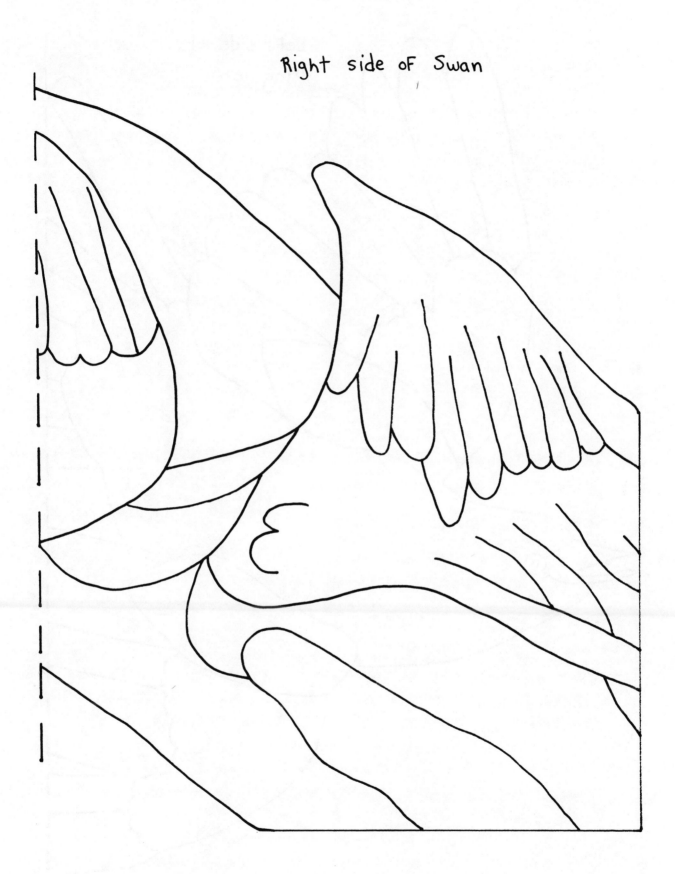

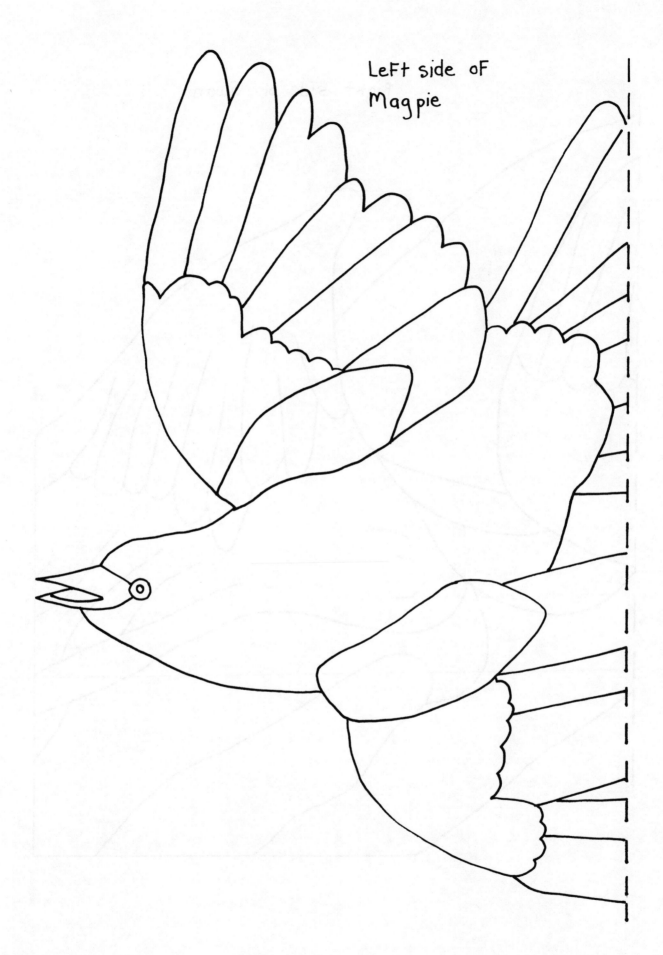

Left side of
Magpie

122

Right side of magpie

123

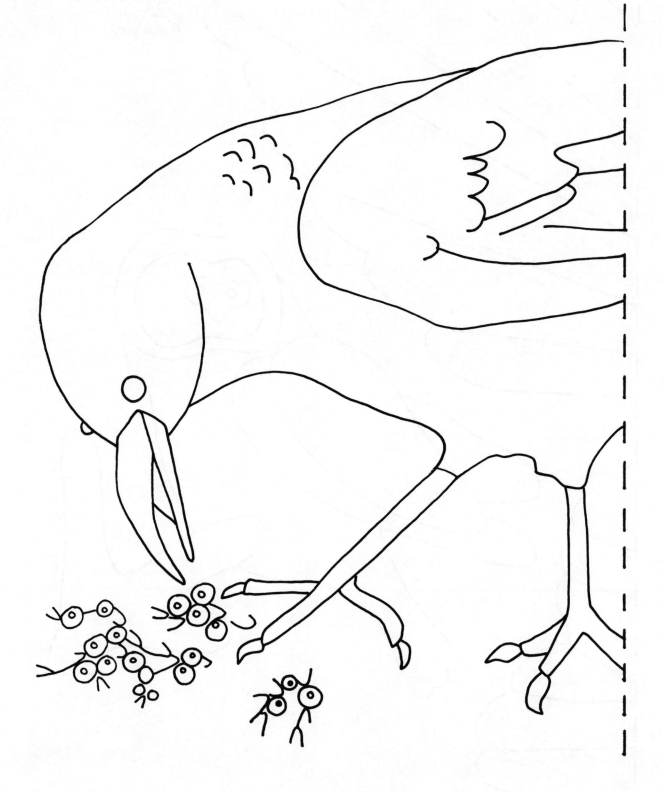

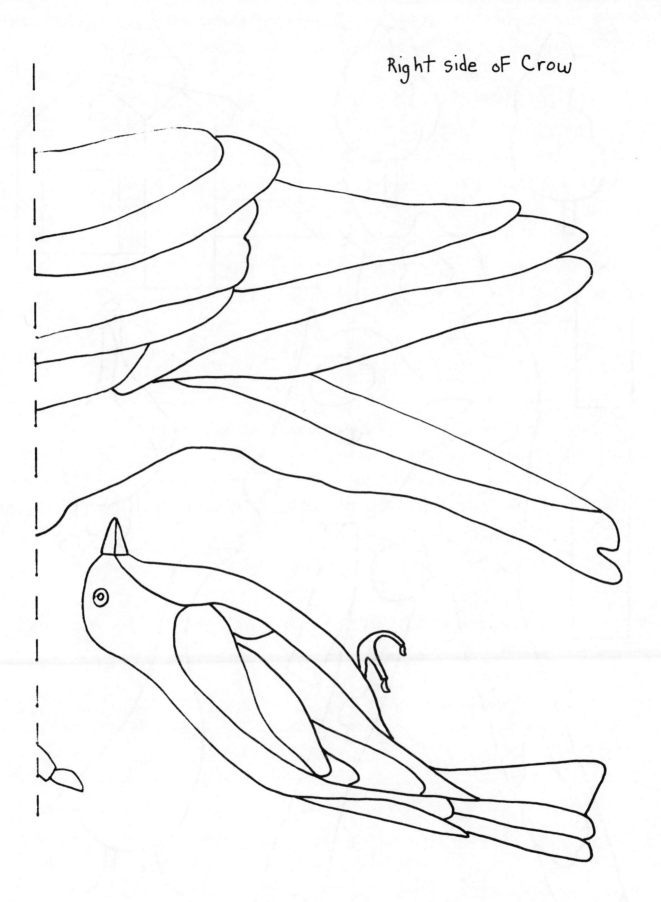

126

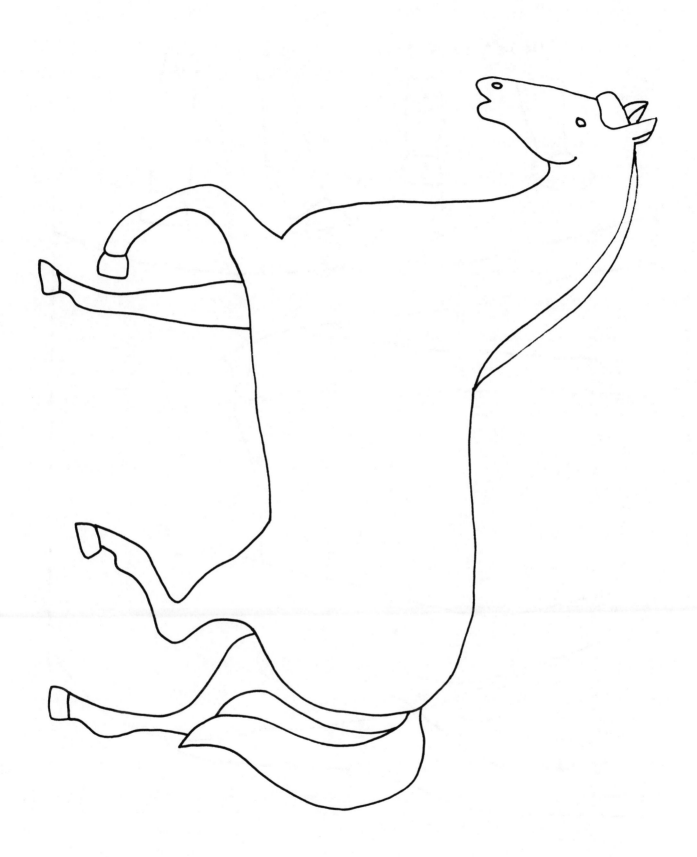

Bottom of Giraffe
Lower Legs

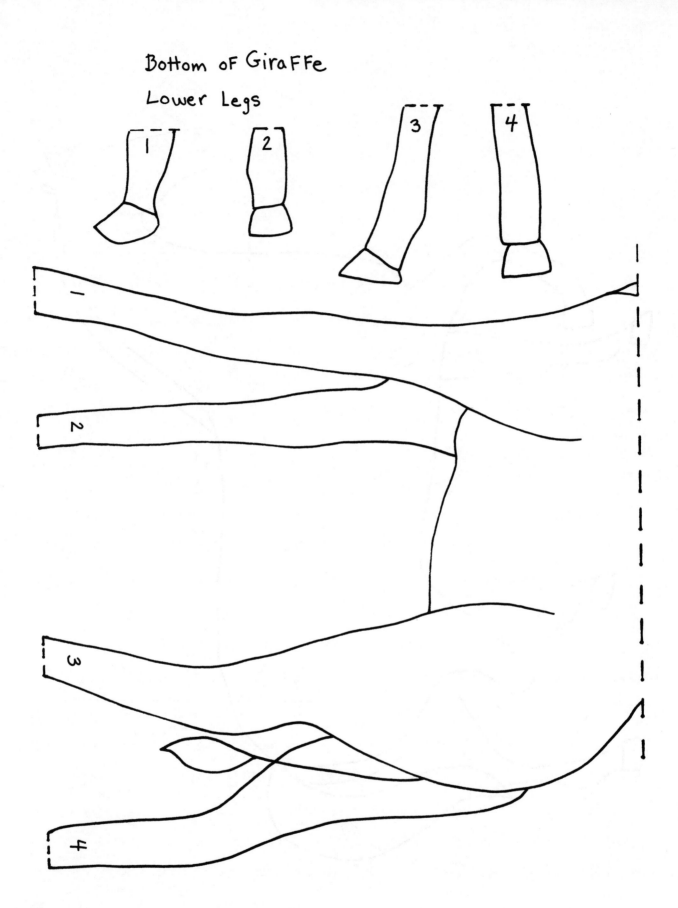

Top of Giraffe

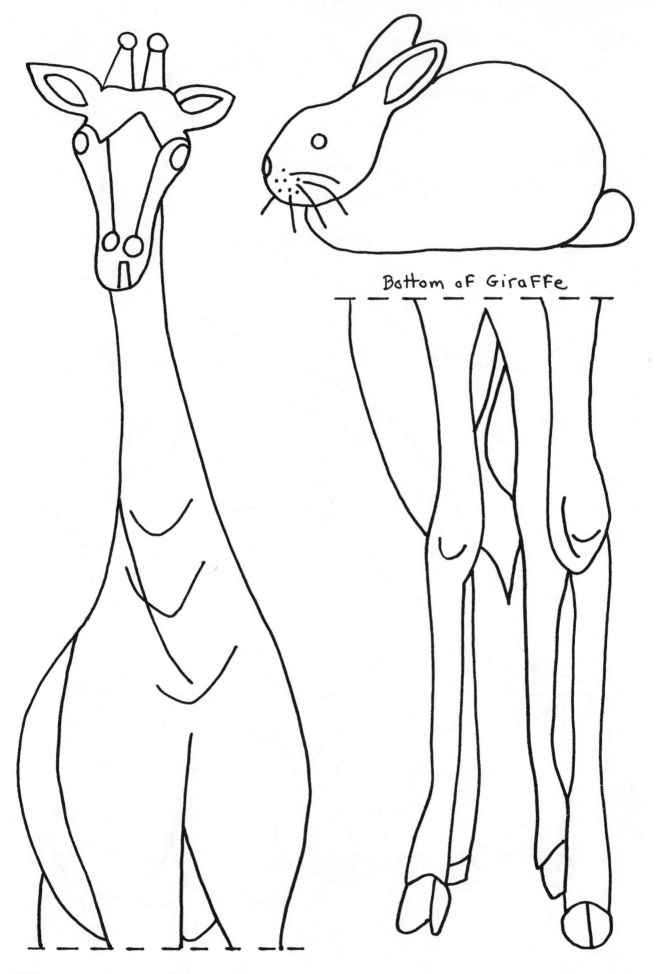

Bottom of Giraffe

133

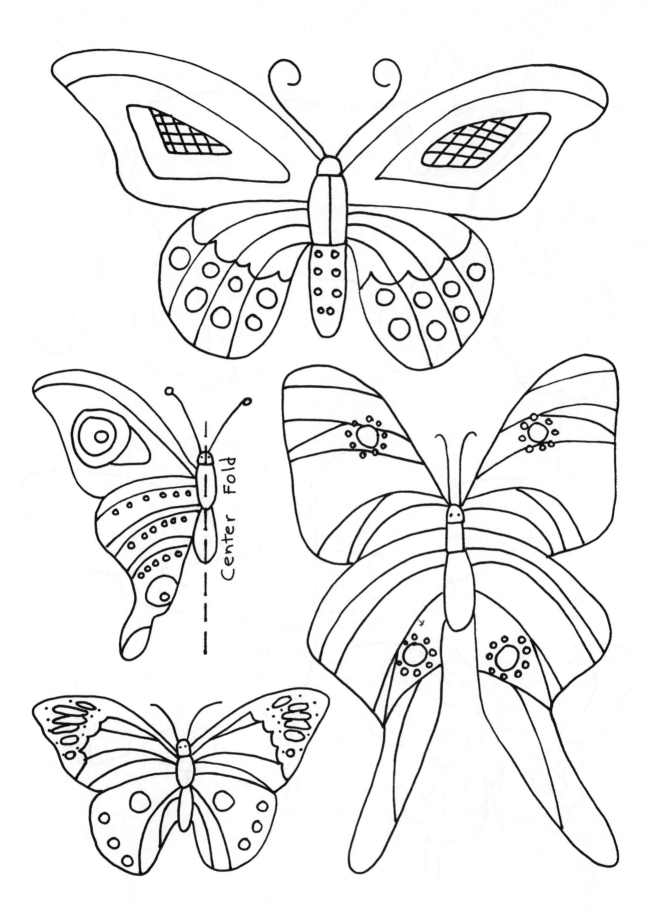

Center Fold

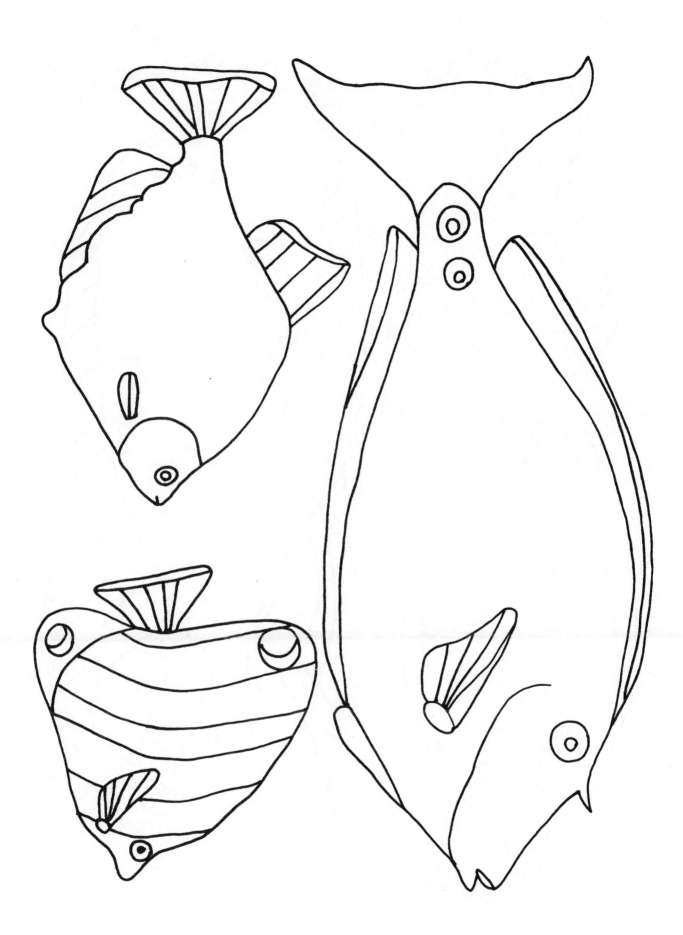

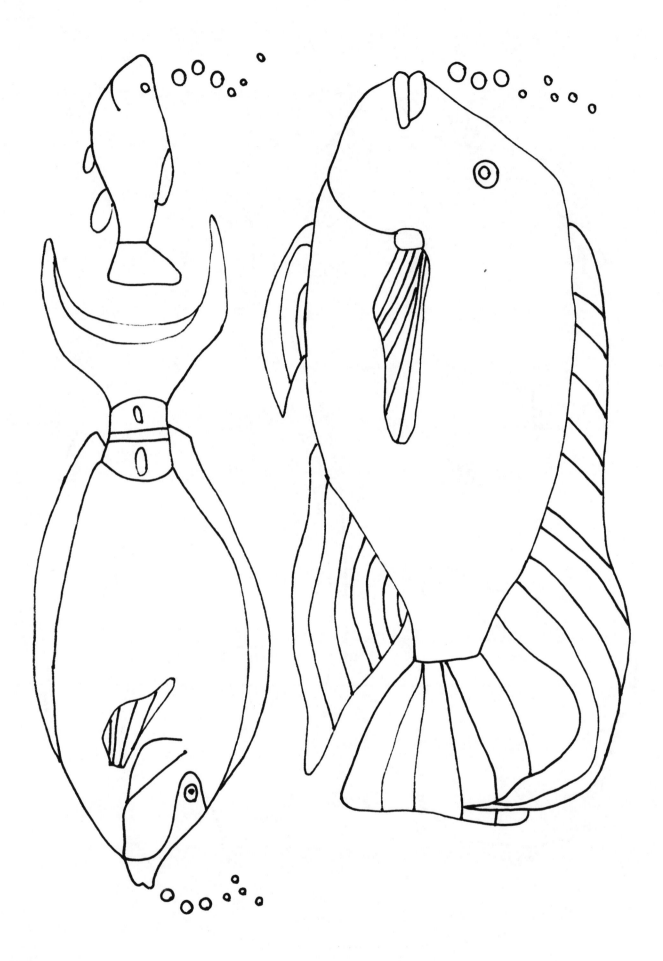

Bottom of
Snowman

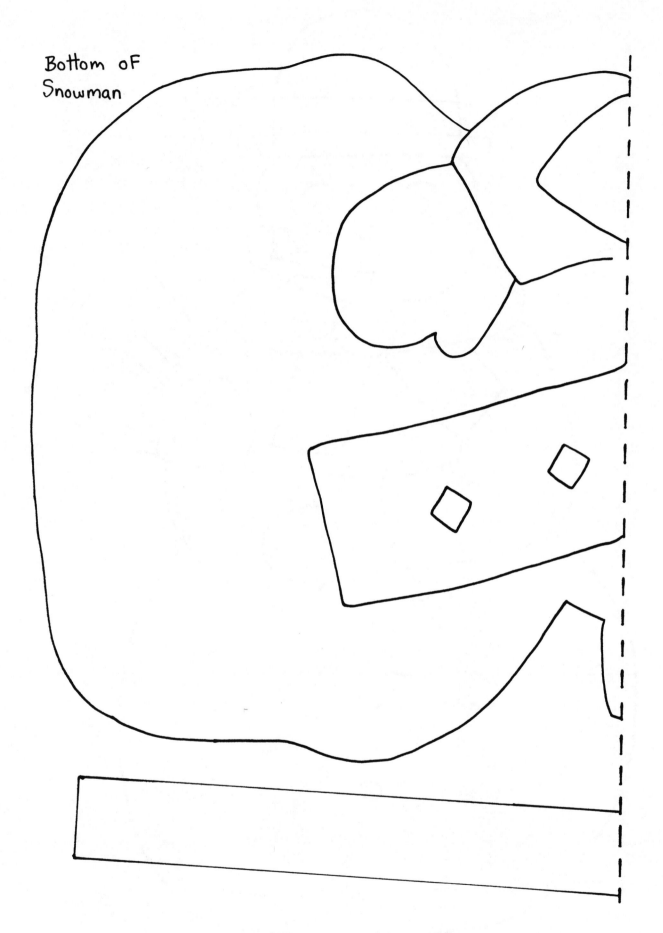

Top of Snowman

Right side of Bow

Bottom of Santa Claus

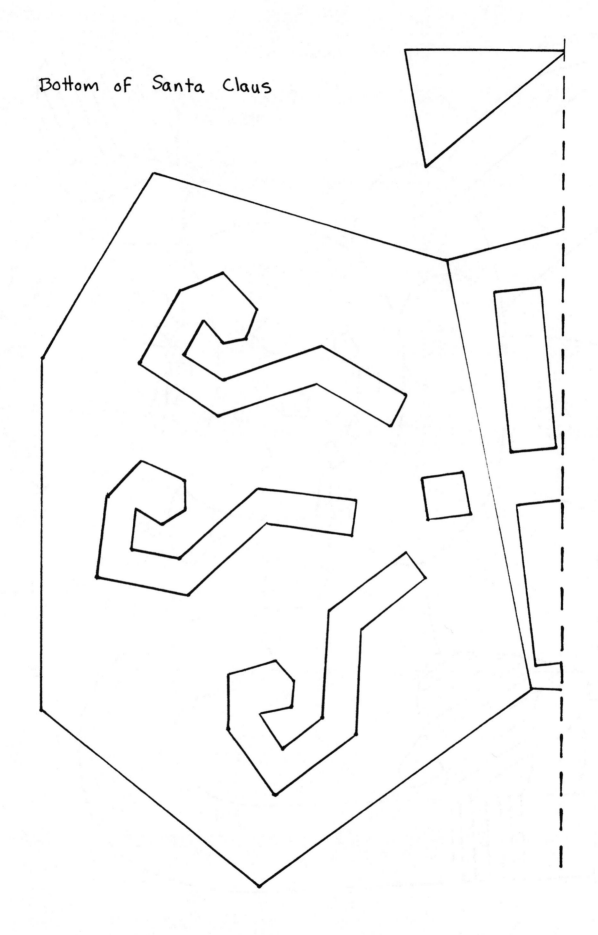

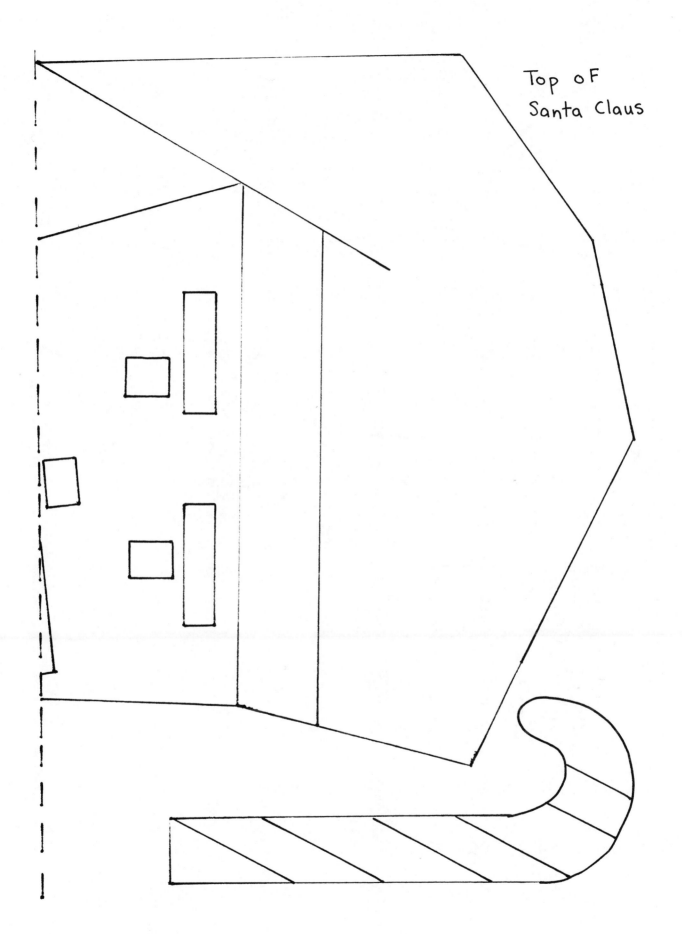

Top of
Santa Claus

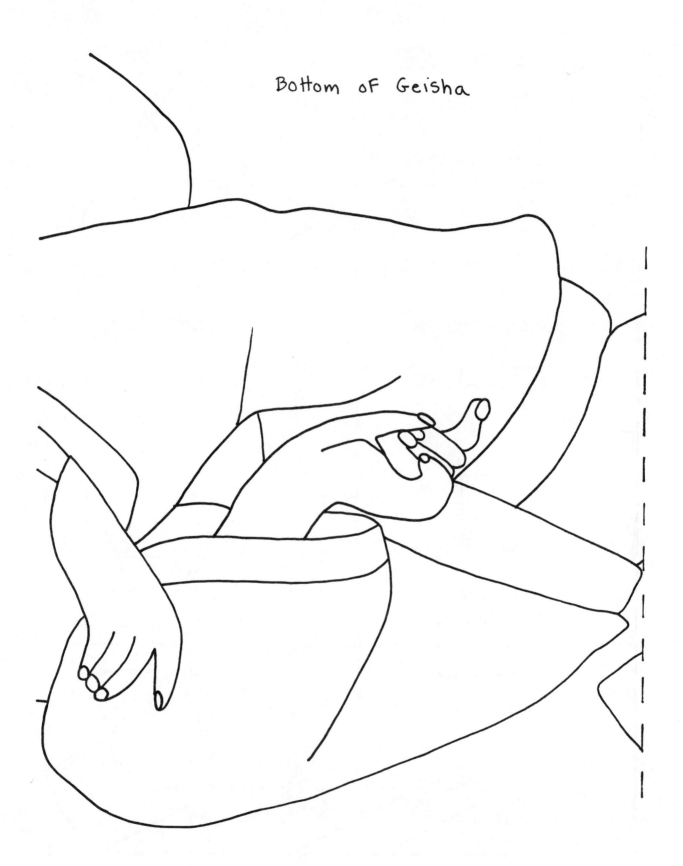

Bottom of Geisha

Top of Geisha

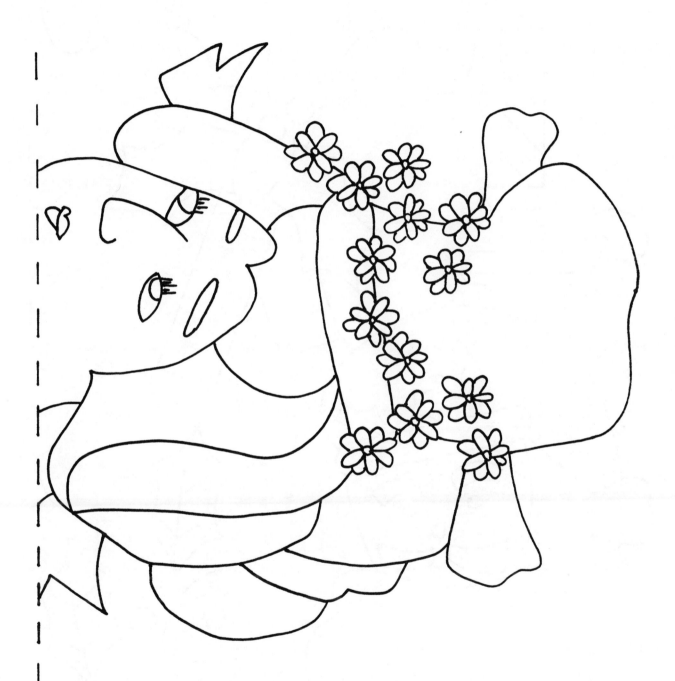

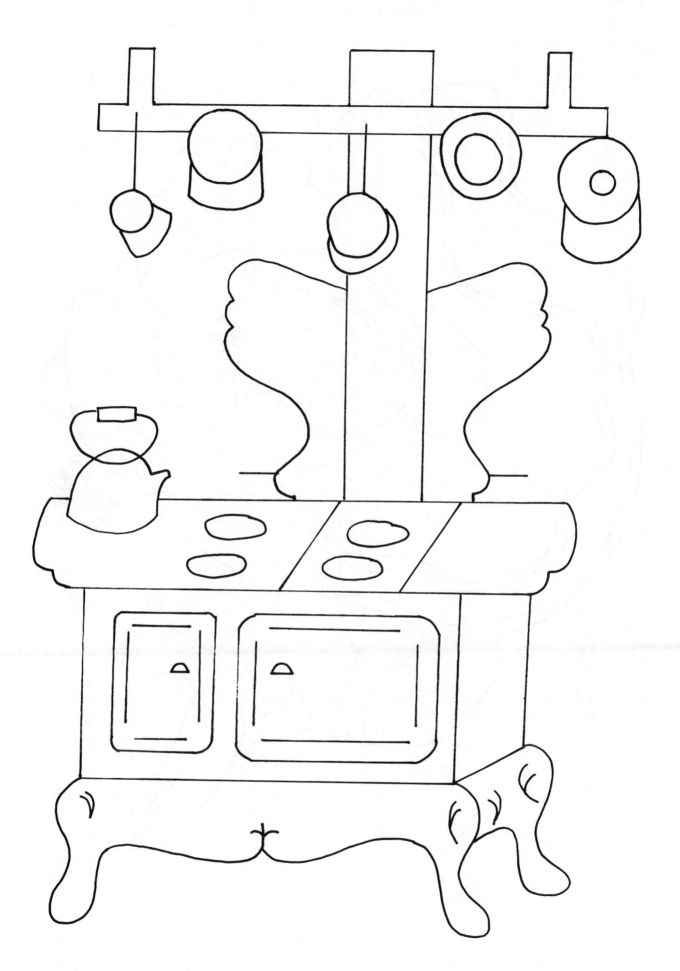

153

Rest
oF Circle

154

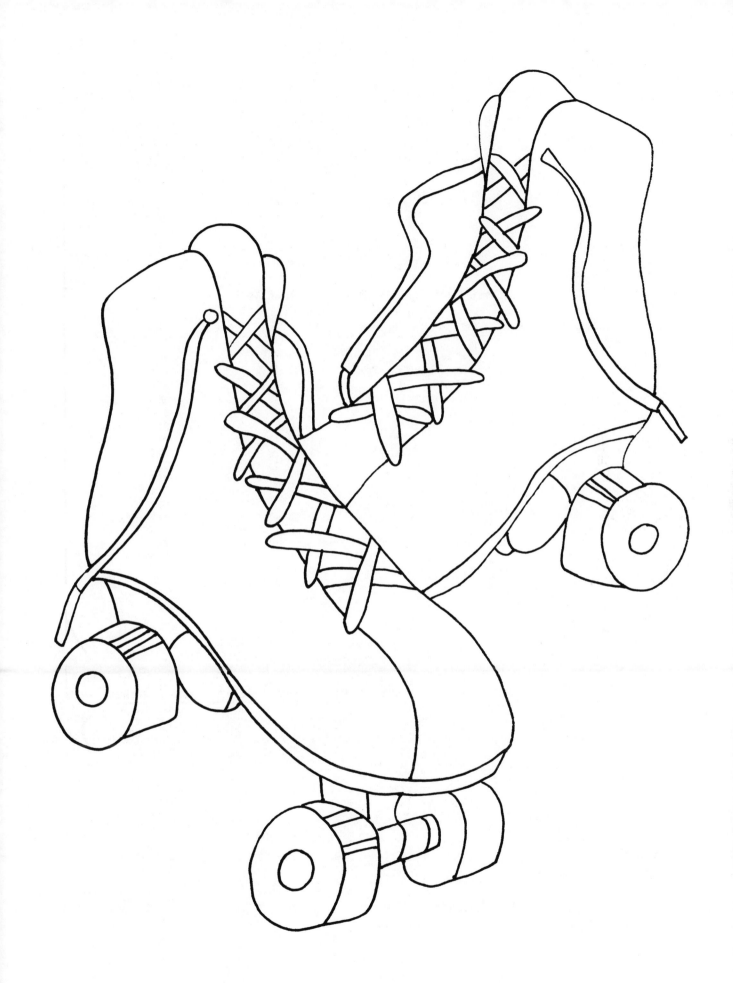

METRIC EQUIVALENCY CHART

MM—MILLIMETRES   CM—CENTIMETRES

INCHES TO MILLIMETRES AND CENTIMETRES

INCHES	MM	CM	INCHES	CM	INCHES	CM
⅛	3	0.3	9	22.9	30	76.2
¼	6	0.6	10	25.4	31	78.7
⅜	10	1.0	11	27.9	32	81.3
½	13	1.3	12	30.5	33	83.8
⅝	16	1.6	13	33.0	34	86.4
¾	19	1.9	14	35.6	35	88.9
⅞	22	2.2	15	38.1	36	91.4
1	25	2.5	16	40.6	37	94.0
1¼	32	3.2	17	43.2	38	96.5
1½	38	3.8	18	45.7	39	99.1
1¾	44	4.4	19	48.3	40	101.6
2	51	5.1	20	50.8	41	104.1
2½	64	6.4	21	53.3	42	106.7
3	76	7.6	22	55.9	43	109.2
3½	89	8.9	23	58.4	44	111.8
4	102	10.2	24	61.0	45	114.3
4½	114	11.4	25	63.5	46	116.8
5	127	12.7	26	66.0	47	119.4
6	152	15.2	27	68.6	48	121.9
7	178	17.8	28	71.1	49	124.5
8	203	20.3	29	73.7	50	127.0

YARDS TO METRES

YARDS	METRES	YARDS	METRES	YARDS	METRES	YARDS	METRES	YARDS	METRES
⅛	0.11	2⅛	1.94	4⅛	3.77	6⅛	5.60	8⅛	7.43
¼	0.23	2¼	2.06	4¼	3.89	6¼	5.72	8¼	7.54
⅜	0.34	2⅜	2.17	4⅜	4.00	6⅜	5.83	8⅜	7.66
½	0.46	2½	2.29	4½	4.11	6½	5.94	8½	7.77
⅝	0.57	2⅝	2.40	4⅝	4.23	6⅝	6.06	8⅝	7.89
¾	0.69	2¾	2.51	4¾	4.34	6¾	6.17	8¾	8.00
⅞	0.80	2⅞	2.63	4⅞	4.46	6⅞	6.29	8⅞	8.12
1	0.91	3	2.74	5	4.57	7	6.40	9	8.23
1⅛	1.03	3⅛	2.86	5⅛	4.69	7⅛	6.52	9⅛	8.34
1¼	1.14	3¼	2.97	5¼	4.80	7¼	6.63	9¼	8.46
1⅜	1.26	3⅜	3.09	5⅜	4.91	7⅜	6.74	9⅜	8.57
1½	1.37	3½	3.20	5½	5.03	7½	6.86	9½	8.69
1⅝	1.49	3⅝	3.31	5⅝	5.14	7⅝	6.97	9⅝	8.80
1¾	1.60	3¾	3.43	5¾	5.26	7¾	7.09	9¾	8.92
1⅞	1.71	3⅞	3.54	5⅞	5.37	7⅞	7.20	9⅞	9.03
2	1.83	4	3.66	6	5.49	8	7.32	10	9.14

INDEX